In memory of
Dad
who took me to church
every Sunday and most Wednesday nights,
discussed the Sunday sermon with his kids,
encouraged us to think about what we believed,
and truly believed that religion was something
to be lived every day of the week.

Clarence Troyer
May 22, 1929 – May 23, 2009

Copyright © 2010 by Joy Troyer
All rights reserved.

Published by
Dyeing Arts Books
2010.
www.DyeingArts.com
Printed in the United States.
ISBN 978-0-9817244-1-6
0-9817244-1-8

Cover art
Batik by Joy Troyer

Printed in the United States of America
Lightning Source

LOOKING FOR TRUTH

Meditations on the Gospels

Joy Troyer

Dyeing Arts Books
California USA

Contents

Introduction 1

The Path to the Holy 4

The Meaning of Christmas 7

The Word Made Flesh 12

Born Again 15

Baptism 18

Wilderness 20

The Lord's Prayer 22

Do Unto Others 25

Do You Want to be Well? 28

Seeds 30

Good Neighbors 33

Life is Good 36

Making Plans 38

Brokenness 40

Forgiving Sins 43

Rich Toward God 45

Worth Saving 48

Rich or Poor   52

Return Rate   55

Who am I?   57

Sinners and Teachers   60

Walking on Water   62

Stay and Rest   65

A Savior   67

Just Talk   70

Someone to Lean On   71

Stuff   73

Prayer   76

What's Love Got to do with it?   78

God Forgives   80

Invitations   82

Saving a Soul   85

Winter   87

Resurrection   89

Introduction

I didn't write this book because of a long-time love for the scriptures. It was actually quite the opposite. I wrote this book because for so long I had ignored (or outright rejected) the idea of any scriptural authority. I had seen scriptures used to judge others, to judge my family and me. I heard scriptures quoted to justify cruelty. I wanted nothing to do with them.

So it made sense that, as an adult, I would join the Unitarian Universalist Church, a denomination in which scripture is seldom used and the writings of Annie Dillard and Joseph Campbell are considered sacred texts. I considered a career in ministry and enrolled at United Seminary of the Twin Cities. The only class that fit into my schedule the first semester was Old Testament, taught by Carolyn Pressler. I was not happy that I had to take this class. But it was required. So, I went. What I found was not the horror stories I had rejected. Dr. Pressler introduced me to the stories of people 4,000 years ago who were amazingly like people I knew. She helped me see the many layers that most of the Bible's stories possess. Instead of trying to explain God by reading the Bible, I looked at the people in these stories and the lessons they had learned about living. And I found that they had much to share. Despite strong faith and direct experience with God, they struggled with life.

It became clear that I did not really want to be a minister. But I loved taking seminary classes. I found myself in long conversations with fellow students, each with a different perspective on the scriptures. I discovered that there was not one single way to read a passage. In fact, I believe that one reason these ancient stories have survived is that of each can be seen in many ways. Our life experiences color these stories so that they touch each of us in differently.

Four years ago I met Michael and it was love at first sight. But Michael was an Orthodox Christian. This was foreign territory for me, completely out of my comfort zone. But in order to spend time with Michael's grandson (Isaiah, the most adorable child on earth), I started attending the St. Nicholas parish. In my new role as "grandma", I sat in the back of the church, playing quietly with a 2-year-old and listening to Father Stephan's sermons. Most weeks they were based on the gospel reading for the day and were about how to live gracious lives. Father Stephan did not spend time making a case for the accuracy of history or in using the Bible to judge others. He just wanted people to live in love.

When my father got cancer, I started a spiritual practice of reading the gospel passage for the upcoming Sunday and writing about it, from wherever I was emotionally that day. Through this process, I realized that in the past I'd been looking for the scriptures to describe my reality and they just didn't. This time, I went to the scriptures looking for truth.

What I found were writings about love, forgiveness, accepting diversity, living simple lives, caring for others, believing in our own abilities, and the worth of all people. As I read and reflected, I often started by looking outward at the problems of the day. However, the scriptures (or perhaps the writing process) moved me to look inward. How could I use these words to improve my world? I began to see the scriptures not as judging, but as nurturing. I found a love for humankind that acknowledged our fragile nature and the immense difficulties of life. But it went beyond sympathy. In these pages is an intense faith in our ability, frail as we may be, to rise above the difficulties and live happy, fulfilling lives that are worthy of celebration. How great is that?

So here I am. My roots are in the Community of Christ Church; a church that taught me that God is still speaking, still revealing God's nature and purposes. I am a member of the Unitarian Universalist denomination, whose principles include acceptance of diversity, the worth of all people, and a search for truth. And my church home is St. Nicholas Russian Orthodox Church, where we celebrate the mystery that is God with music and ritual. These three very different traditions guide my thoughts as I read the scriptures. I am sure that there are other religions that see these scriptures differently. But my hope is that my perspective may open the scriptures to those who have found them difficult. Perhaps they will recognize the wisdom and love that our ancestors have passed on in these scriptures and accept the help they offer as we struggle to live gracious lives in a mad world.

The Path to the Holy

Matthew 1:1-16
The book of the generation of Jesus Christ, the son of David, the son of Abraham. Abraham begat Isaac; and Isaac begat Jacob.

> I've heard of them. Everyone's heard of them. Good men. Men in touch with God. Of course they are in this list. A good beginning to the lineage of the Son of God.

And Jacob begat Judas and his brethren.

> Judas? Obviously not THE Judas.
> Have I heard of this Judas? I don't think so.

And Judas begat Phares and Zara of Thamar; and Phares begat Esrom; and Esrom begat Aram; and Aram begat Aminadab; and Aminadab begat Naasson; and Naason begat Salmon.

> Who are these people? Maybe they are the normal folks, the ones who kept things running day to day, who taught their children to be honest and fair, the ones no one could do without even if they didn't make it into the history books. They are part of the path, perhaps the biggest part.

And Salmon begat Booz of Rachab; and Booz begat Obed of Ruth.

> A Woman! And a foreign woman at that! Yes, it takes all kinds to pave the path to great things. If Ruth had not followed her mother-in-law to Bethlehem, we might not have had Jesus. Think of that!

And Obed begat Jesse and Jesse begat David the king.

> Royalty is in this path. Good blood, perhaps enriching the normal blood. This perks up the line a bit.

And David begat Solomon of her that had been the wife of Urias.

> Royal blood, but not so honorable blood, this David who had Urias sent off to war and certain death so that he could have his wife.

And Solomon begat Roboam; and Roboam begat Abia and Abia begat Asa; and Asa begat Josaphat; and Josaphat begat Joram; and Joram begat Ozias; and Ozias begat Joatham; and Joatham begat Achaz; and Achaz begat Ezekias; and Ezekias begat Manasses; and Manasses begat Amon; and Amon begat Josias; and Josias begat Jechonias and his brethren, about the time they were carried away to Babylon:

> This is a long path. It takes many years and many people. Why so long? Perhaps the path to the holy requires some hard lessons along the way (defeat, banishment, adjustment to change) before we can see the holy in others; before we realize we need a savior.

And after they were brought to Babylon, Jechonias begat Salathiel; and Salathiel begat Zorobabel; and Zorobabel begat Abiud; and Abiud begat Eliakim; and Eliakim begat Azor; and Azor begat Sadoc; and Sadoc begat Achim; and Achim begat Eliud; and Eliud begat Eleazar; and Eleazar begat Matthan; and Mattan begat Jacob; and Jacob begat Joseph the husband of Mary, of whom was born Jesus, who is called Christ.

> But Joseph isn't even related to Jesus. We went through this entire lineage to get to the adoptive father of Jesus?

> We are all entrusted with children, sent to us with a spark of the holy. They come to us, unworthy as we are; our history spattered with kings and thieves, men of honor and men of mischief. And we attempt to guide them, though they seem guided from within. We tell them the stories of our beginnings so they will feel grounded. We tell them stories of our kings, so they will have pride. We tell them stories of our exiles and our homecoming, so they will have hope. We recount the story of the foreigner so they

will adjust to change. We tell the stories of our mistakes so that, just perhaps, they will not make the same ones-- though we know they will make many of their own. And we tell the story of Jesus, so they will know that they are holy and precious from the day they were born; that they are full of potential, no matter what their bloodline, no matter how lowly their beginnings.

We are all part of the path our children walk. None of us can be hidden and none should be. When it is all said and done, the begats just take us so far. Each of us moves ahead, making the next section of the path, using the pride, hope, and potential we have been given by those who have gone before.

The Meaning of Christmas

I have celebrated Christmas ever since I can remember. It has been a time of wonder, presents, and tradition. Each Christmas, Dad would sit by the tree and read the story from Luke. But over the years, my religious beliefs wavered. I had serious doubts about the virgin birth, the existence of angels, and the historical reality of Jesus. I read birth stories of other religious deities that sounded a lot like the Christian account. I found it hard to accept the Christmas story as "real." The other parts of the holiday season became more stressful. It seemed I was frazzled for no reason. It was not a happy time!

One day I found myself saying that the Christmas story, for me, was just a myth. But as I said it, I realized that if it were a myth, there must be a reason for it. Why would people tell this story over and over for so many years? It must have some meaning, some truth to divulge, some message to bring. So I looked again at the stories in Luke and Matthew. This time, instead of looking for reality, I looked for truth.

Luke 1:26-33
The angel Gabriel was sent from God unto a city of Galilee named Nazareth, to a virgin espoused to a man whose name was Joseph, of the house of David; and the virgin's name was Mary. And the angel came unto her, and said, "Hail, thou that art highly favoured, the Lord is with thee: blessed art thou among women. ... And, behold, thou shalt conceive in thy womb, and bring forth a son, and shalt call his name Jesus. He shall be great, and shall be called the Son of the Highest: and the Lord God shall give unto him the throne of his father David: And he shall reign over the house of Jacob for ever; and of his kingdom there shall be no end."

Christmas is a time to celebrate the miracle of new life. It is a miracle beyond understanding. Most of the mothers I know talk about how amazing it is to feel new life stirring within them. It is hard to believe that a healthy child is not a gift from God. But the joining of Mary and

God represents more than just the birth of a child. The divine touches us in unexpected ways to produce new life of all sorts. The moment of the divine touch may not manifest itself for some time. We often need time to understand and let the divine work within us for a while. But we often have a sense of something coming. Something good.

Mary's story helps us understand the meaning of Christmas.

Let us celebrate Christmas by recognizing that the divine is working within each of us to produce new ideas and new insights; that wonderful new things are coming. The evergreens of Christmas help us remember that life and new growth can lie dormant through the winter. But the green reminds us that spring with its new life will come.

Luke 2:6-7
And so it was, that, while they were there, the days were accomplished that she should be delivered. And she brought forth her firstborn son, and wrapped him in swaddling clothes, and laid him in a manger; because there was no room for them in the inn.

New life, new energy, new hope, and new ideas do not wait for a sunny day when we have planned to have time to properly ponder and admire them. Newness springs up around us at the most unusual times: when we are traveling, when we fulfilling other obligations, when we are tired and trying to sleep. But there it is, something new and wonderful. We hold the new thought, the new child, the new insight close to us, nurturing it the best we can at the time, wondering where this will lead.

The story of the divine child in the manger helps us understand the meaning of Christmas.

Let us celebrate Christmas by watching for new insights, new life, and new hope in unexpected places. May the crèche, though now so familiar, remind us that the divine shows up in unexpected places.

Luke 2:8-14
And there were in the same country shepherds abiding in the field, keeping watch over their flock by night. And, lo, the angel of the Lord came upon them, and the glory of the Lord shone round about them: and they were sore afraid. And the angel said unto them, "Fear not: for, behold, I bring you good tidings of great joy, which shall be to all people. For unto you is born this day in the city of David a Savior, which is Christ the Lord."

And suddenly there was with the angel a multitude of the heavenly host, praising God and saying, "Glory to God in the highest, and on earth peace, good will toward men."

When the divine works within us to produce new life, that is reason to celebrate! I believe that, just as in the story of Jesus, each of us is a child of God, a product of the divine and the human, a person of great potential and the cause of great heavenly celebration! If there are angels, I believe they sing each time a new person is born, each time a new idea is discovered, each time we show divine creativity and make progress toward peace on earth.

The story of the shepherds and the angels help us understand the meaning of Christmas.

Let us celebrate Christmas by recognizing the divine nature of each person. The candles of Christmas with their solid base and burning flame remind us of this sacred union of the human and the divine.

Matthew 2:1-8
Now when Jesus was born in Bethlehem of Judea in the days of Herod the king, behold there came wise men from the east to Jerusalem, Saying, "Where is he that is born King of the Jews? For we have seen his star in the east and are come to worship him." When Herod the king had heard these things, he was troubled, and all Jerusalem with him. And when he had gathered all the chief

priests and scribes of the people together, he demanded of them where Christ should be born. And they said unto him, "In Bethlehem of Judea; for thus it is written by the prophet..."

Then Herod, when he had privily called the wise men, enquired of them diligently what time the star appeared. And he sent them to Bethlehem, and said, "Go and search diligently for the young child; and when ye have found him, bring me word again, that I may come and worship him also."

Those in power are often afraid of new life. Newborn babies, though small and physically weak, come to us so free of loyalty to tradition, so free of entrenched ways, so free to come up with their own ideas. Herod tried to stop this new power by killing the babies. But it can't be stopped. We can't keep things the way they are. The new children, the new ideas, the new creativity, the new insights just keep coming.

The story of Herod helps us understand the meaning of Christmas.

Let us celebrate Christmas by embracing new ideas (rather than being afraid of them), by letting go of our need for power and instead embrace the wonderful and diverse gifts that others have to offer. Perhaps the symbol of the star that shines for everyone can help us remember that our own power is enhanced when we share it with others.

Matthew 2:9-11
When they had heard the king, they departed; and, lo, the star, which they saw in the east, went before them, till it came and stood over where the young child was. When they saw the star, they rejoiced with exceeding great joy. And when they were come into the house, they saw the young child with Mary his mother, and fell down, and worshipped him: and when they had opened their treasures, they presented unto him gifts; gold, and frankincense, and myrrh.

The wise know that new life is something to be sought out and cherished, not something to be killed or avoided. The wise understand that new life needs to be nurtured and supported; that only by investing in these new lives, these new ideas, will they both grow and live truly divine lives.

The story of the wise men helps us understand the meaning of Christmas.

Let us celebrate Christmas by seeking out newness and helping to nurture and support it in its many forms. The Christmas present symbolizes these gifts of nurture and support.

There is, in this story of Jesus' birth, quite a bit of truth and meaning, even for those of us who find its history hard to accept. It is a story about recognizing the divine within and around us, in unexpected places. It is about appreciating diversity and learning to embrace new things. It is about nurturing new life and new ideas. It is about change and celebration.

Let us celebrate the birth of Jesus by giving birth to a new idea, looking with wider vision, working toward change.

In the season of giving, let us support and nurture those institutions that courageously recognize that all life is divine, that work to acknowledge and change oppressive systems.

And as we await the birth of the divine, let us be open to the divine in those around us who we may have overlooked or discounted.

Advent season is indeed a time of anticipation, for the new ideas that will move the world in a new direction are soon to be born.

The Word Made Flesh

John 1:1-14
In the beginning was the Word, and the Word was with God, and the Word was God. The same was in the beginning with God. All things were made by him; and without him was not any thing made that was made. In him was life; and the life was the light of men. And the light shineth in darkness; and the darkness comprehended it not. There was a man sent from God, whose name was John. The same came for a witness, to bear witness of the Light, that all men through him might believe. He was not that Light, but was sent to bear witness of that Light. That was the true Light, which lighteth every man that cometh into the world. He was in the world, and the world was made by him, and the world knew him not. He came unto his own, and his own received him not. But as many as received him, to them gave he power to become the sons of God, even to them that believe on his name: Which were born not of blood, nor of the will of the flesh, nor of the will of man, but of God. And the Word was made flesh, and dwelt among us, and we beheld his glory, the glory as of the only begotten of the Father, full of grace and truth.

Every Sunday I go to church at St. Nicholas Orthodox Church with my husband, Michael. This was not something I ever expected to do. After my first visit to St. Nicholas, I did not expect to ever feel at home there. I was raised in the Community of Christ Church, a small Christian denomination, one that is relatively young in religious terms; established in the United States less than 200 years ago. From there I moved to the Unitarian Universalists, a group that does not consider itself Christian (though they are not actively opposed to it.) Both are pretty "Protestant" in practice. The congregation sits, then stands for a hymn or two. There is little pomp, almost nothing in the way of ornament or ritual.

In contrast, the Orthodox Church is an ancient tradition, a true "smells and bells" religion, rich with music, incense, chanting, icons, robes, and ritual. It is about as different from anything in my previous experience as any church could be. But I am there, Sunday after Sunday.

I started going to be with my grandson, Isaiah. I could give him my attention while Michael attended to his own spiritual needs. I could distract Isaiah with toys and still enjoy the music and beauty of the service. I could justify my presence there, but I would not allow myself to kiss the icons or make the sign of the cross. These were just too far outside of my comfort zone.

When Isaiah was 3, I started helping with the preschool class. The first thing the teacher showed the kids was how to make the Sign of the Cross. She held up her right thumb. "God the Father," she stated. Then she held up her index finger. "God the Son." And the middle finger. "God the Holy Spirit." She put the three fingers together and with them, she touched her forehead. "In the name of the Father…" She touched her stomach. "…and the Son." She touched first her right shoulder. "…and the Holy Spirit." And finally her left shoulder. "Amen." We all repeated it and helped the children follow the instructions.

I, too, touched my forehead. God the Father. God is in my head. The God that is logical and responsible. The parent who makes sure there is enough for everyone, stresses over problems and looks for ways to resolve them. The God of strength and patience.

I touched my stomach. God the Son. God is in my being, my gut, my heart. The God that is creative, emotional, and vibrant. The son who laughs at silly faces, delights in helium balloons, fights against restraint and cries at the death of a pet. The God of faith and beauty.

I touched my shoulders. God the Holy Spirit. God is in my arms, reaching outside myself to do for others. The servant that sees others' needs and works to make the world a better place. The God of love and charity.

Amen.

The Orthodox make a final gesture at the end of the sign of the cross. They touch the ground. God is right here, in this place, right now.

The word was made flesh for me in that moment. The ancient words of John bore witness to me that God was in the world, through me. Hearing the gospel as taught to preschoolers broke through my own darkness. As I went back into church, I witnessed God in each person there as they reverently touched their head, their heart, their arms, and the ground. I hesitantly made, for the first time in my life, the Sign of the Cross. And I felt a little more able to bear witness to the holy, ready to spread a little light.

Born Again

John 3:1-15
There was a man of the Pharisees, named Nicodemus, a ruler of Jews: The same came to Jesus by night and said unto him, "Rabbi, we know that thou art a teacher come from God: for no man can do these miracles that thou doest, except God be with him." Jesus answered and said unto him, "Verily, verily, I say unto thee, except a man be born again, he cannot see the kingdom of God." Nicodemus said unto him, "How can a man be born when he is old? Can he enter the second time into his mother's womb and be born?" Jesus answered, "Verily, verily, I say unto thee, except a man be born of water and of the Spirit, he cannot enter into the kingdom of God. That which is born of the flesh is flesh; and that which is born of the Spirit is spirit. Marvel not that I said unto thee, 'Ye must be born again.' The wind bloweth where it listeth, and thou hearest the sound thereof, but can not tell whence it cometh, and whither it goeth: so is every one that is born of the Spirit." Nicodemus answered and said unto him, "How can these things be?" Jesus answered and said unto him, "Art thou a master of Israel, and knowest not these things? Verily, verily, I say unto thee, we speak that we do know, and testify that we have seen; and ye receive not our witness. If I have told you earthly things, and ye believe not, how shall ye believe, if I tell you of heavenly things? And no man hath ascended up to heaven, but he that came down from heaven, even the Son of man which is in heaven. And as Moses lifted up the serpent in the wilderness, even so must the Son of man be lifted up: That whosoever believeth in him should not perish, but have eternal life."

Born again. That's a phrase that, for me, has come to be associated with proselytizing. People who are so sure that I need to be baptized-- well, they scare me a little. My "fight or flight" reflex kicks in when the phrase "born again" is uttered. But that really isn't fair. When I think about it, to be born again would be to start over with one's thoughts, habits, ideas--to rethink everything. We aren't born with language, culture, or religion. We learn as we grow. To be born again of water and spirit would be to wipe the slate clean and consider anew the nature and spirit of things. Perhaps this is something to contemplate.

At a workshop for group facilitators, the leader divided us into two groups and put us in separate rooms. I knew none of the 10 or so women in my group. The leader asked our group to develop a four-word sign language vocabulary. She explained that in our culture, nuance was primary. We did not need broad strokes to convey messages. We respected personal space and kept our distance out of that respect. So, we developed our four subtle signs: one each for four simple phrases often used in casual conversation. In silence, we practiced our signs, walking around and meeting each other. We smiled and laughed at our silly silent language.

After about 15 minutes, we were joined by the second group who had also developed signs for the same four phrases. We used no words, only our signs. As you might expect, their "culture" was much different than ours. They used their whole body, coming close to meet new friends. Within minutes, maybe seconds, I felt uncomfortable. These people were garish, offensive, disrespectful, and without shame. I stopped "talking" with the new group and went back to "my own people." I used my subtle signs to indicate my dislike for these wild people.

After only about 10 minutes, the leader sat us down with a large piece of paper between us and asked us to describe the other group. I knew how I felt about them. To my surprise, Group Two thought our group was snobby, aloof, inhospitable, even mean. With only a couple exceptions, the participants felt much more comfortable with their "own kind." And all this developed in a matter of about 30 minutes among complete strangers. I was embarrassed at my ability to so quickly label a whole group as "obnoxious," to reject so easily and with so little at stake. Imagine the walls I must have built up in real life after years of cultural teaching, family systems, language nuances, and personal experience. I swore to be more tolerant, to recognize that actions could be seen and interpreted from many points of view. And occasionally I have some success.

To be born again, I think, would mean to look beyond the inbred training, to imagine ourselves as infants looking around in awe at a whole world of new experience – all of it potentially good. Could we imagine ourselves growing up with different parents, different holidays, different favorite foods, different expectations? Sometimes I try to imagine growing up male or black or rich or homeless. Frankly, success in this is (and can only be) pretty limited. But what this exercise does is help me realize that my view is not definitive. If I had grown up in different circumstances, I would view things differently. What is "aloof" to one person may be "respectful" to another. I begin to believe in the goodness of others.

On my best days, I try to look with fresh eyes and believe that each person (each "son of man") is potentially offering me a hand of friendship, if only I will recognize it. I try to refrain from being defensive and judgmental. It isn't easy. This "born again" thing is tough. I am dependent upon others to help me understand. As I venture into unknown territory, I am sometimes confused or even afraid. And sometimes I just am not strong enough. I retreat back into my comfort zone. But when I persevere, I discover beauty I had not known existed. When I am born again, I glimpse the Kingdom of God.

Baptism

Matthew 3:13-17
Then cometh Jesus from Galilee to Jordan unto John to be baptized of him. But John forbad him, saying, " I have need to be baptized of thee, and comest thou to me?" And Jesus answering said unto him, "Suffer it to be so now: for thus it becometh us to fulfill all righteousness." Then he suffered him. And Jesus, when he was baptized, went up straightway out of the water: and, lo, the heavens were opened unto him, and he saw the Spirit of God descending like a dove, and lighting upon him: And lo a voice from heaven, saying, "This is my beloved Son, in whom I am well pleased."

What does it mean to be baptized?
Can we be washed clean?
Can we be born again?
To start over, this time moving in a different direction?
For that to happen,
I have to admit that I am imperfect,
That my current agenda may need some tweaking.
I have to be willing to change some things,
Negative things that have come to define me.
To let go and look at life in a new way.
I must be willing to confess my need to be cleansed.

Shall I go into the waters of baptism?
What would that require of me?
To believe.
To really believe that it mattered.
To be willing to make a fresh start.
To change my agenda.

Who can perform this rite of washing?
Whose power is required?
Someone who believes that it matters,
Who believes that new beginnings are possible.

Even for sinners.
Even for me.

It takes a humble confessor.
One who believes that it is possible to move beyond the past.
One who loves the world enough to look beyond what is.
One who trusts that there are those who will allow this movement.
One who is strong enough to ask for baptism.

It takes a humble servant.
One who sees the divinity amid our imperfections.
One who knows the power of forgiveness.
One who believes their act of washing may change the world.
One who is strong enough to act.

And when the servant and confessor act together
To move forward with loving eyes and forgiving hearts,
We find God.

Wilderness

Matthew 4
Then Jesus was led up by the Spirit into the wilderness to be tempted by the devil. He fasted forty days and forty nights, and afterwards he was famished.

The tempter came and said to him, "If you are the Son of God, command these stones to become loaves of bread." But he answered, "It is written, 'One does not live by bread alone, but by every word that comes from the mouth of God.'" Then the devil took him to the holy city and placed him on the pinnacle of the temple, saying to him, "If you are the Son of God, throw yourself down; for it is written, 'He will command his angels concerning you,' and 'On their hands they will bear you up, so that you will not dash your foot against a stone.'" Jesus said to him, "Again it is written, 'Do not put the Lord your God to the test.'" Again, the devil took him to a very high mountain and showed him all the kingdoms of the world and their splendor; and he said to him, "All these I will give you, if you will fall down and worship me." Jesus said to him, "Away with you, Satan! For it is written, 'Worship the Lord your God, and serve only him.'" Then the devil left him, and suddenly angels came and waited on him.

Here I am. In the wilderness. A wilderness paved with city streets, lighted by billboards saying, "If you are a child of God, you deserve the best. Stop here for the meal of your life. The price is reasonable. You have it in your power. Think of it: pancakes with melted butter and pecans. Or a café latte (decaf if you prefer, with cinnamon, light on the foam) with chocolate croissants and the company of sophisticated professionals and graduate students. We can treat your taste buds to the experience of a lifetime, topped off with a vintage wine. Just put it on your credit card." Suddenly my life of macaroni and cheese, Diet Coke and ham sandwiches seems boring. I am special. I am a child of God, made in God's image. I deserve the food of the Gods. Maybe. At least once in a while. I'm so hungry. Surely God intends for me to enjoy these things.

Here I am. In the wilderness. A wilderness with too many bosses and irritating people. Of bills and mortgage payments. Of long commutes and short deadlines. I work hard and never have enough. The TV shows me "affordable" luxury cars and beach vacations for any budget. The boss offers a promotion. More hours, but great pay. I could fire the irritating coworker. I could afford the condo in Italy. It could all be mine. For a mere 60 hours a week. I'm doing it for the kids. Really, I am. They deserve the best.

Here I am. In the wilderness. A wilderness of needy family, needy friends, needy homeless, needy employees, needy governments. The needs never stop. But I am a child of God. I have needs, too. Inside my brain are voices saying, "Make them take care of me for a while. If I cry, or pout, or sigh deeply, they will do my bidding. It's my turn. For one day, let them come to me." But will one day be enough? And what of their needs?

Here I am. In the wilderness. And suddenly I notice the flowers along the paved streets. I hear laughter in my office. I see children playing with simple boxes in tiny yards, unaware that they should have more things. I see dancing clouds above the freeways, providing performance art to the weary commuters. I see smiles from those I help and feel the spirit swell inside me. I haven't moved, but I am no longer in the wilderness. The angels have lifted me up and waited on me.

The Lord's Prayer

Matthew 6:9-13
After this manner therefore pray ye: Our Father which art in heaven, Hallowed be thy name. Thy kingdom come, Thy will be done on earth, as it is in heaven. Give us this day our daily bread. And forgive us our debts, as we forgive our debtors. And lead us not into temptation, but deliver us from evil: For thine is the kingdom, and the power, and the glory, forever. Amen.

I'm not a big believer in a listening God. I have seen too many horrors, experienced too much sadness, to believe that there is a God who listens to prayer and grants the worthy their wishes. But I do believe in the power of prayer. I believe that it is good for us to reach into our souls and admit to a higher power that we are not able to do it all on our own. The Lord's Prayer is a template.

It starts by recognizing that there is a power outside ourselves, a power worthy of reverence. I need to do that from time to time. I am not the center of all that is important, but neither am I alone. I really don't know what "God" is or how God works. God is a great big mystery. But when I look around me, see the blooming flowers, the glistening snow, the jumping of my grandson, the constant waves on the beach, the music of Beethoven, the guitar riffs of Carlos Santana, the art of Monet, the smell of coffee, the wonder of science… well, I just can't believe there isn't something that holds us all together into something wild with potential. Something hallowed. And my prayer is sent out to this something. And when I send the prayer out, I feel connected, nurtured and blessed.

When I put myself into this hallowed space, surrounded by creation and creativity, the possibility of a heavenly kingdom seems valid. If I were able to pull from this immense energy and beauty, instead of looking only to my one, small human body, perhaps the task would not seem so daunting.

The next part is hard. I don't have a clue as to what God is, so God's will is really a mystery. "Thy will be done." What does that mean? I can only guess. But my prayer did not start with this request. It started by connecting with a greater power. It started by going to a hallowed place. So, my guess starts from this space, where I recognize that I am one part of a whole. When I try to follow God's will, I have no choice but to consider that whole, and do my best to contribute to its grandeur, its hallowedness.

In the midst of this power and glory, the prayer contains a request for daily sustenance. A prayer for the most basic of needs. Daily bread. Sometimes I forget this. In my attempt to change the world, to be important, I forget to take care of myself. I need this reminder.

As I sit in this hallowed space, finding energy from others, making sure my basic needs are met, it is nearly impossible to comprehend the vast wealth I have received from others. Whether valid or not, I feel unworthy, in debt to this world and this mysterious God. It is easy to dwell in this attitude of unworthiness, a deer in the headlights waiting for the oncoming truck to deliver my just punishment. But if I stay there, focused on my faults, reliving my mistakes, then I am not going to help build this kingdom that moments ago felt possible. I need forgiveness, permission to move ahead despite my inability to even the balance, knowing that I will always receive more than I can give. Once forgiven, I must take that blessing and forgive those who may not have the ability to repay me.

It is always a good idea to think about the possible pitfalls ahead. Though I don't think God leads us into evil places, I think God requires us to think carefully about the path we take. A regular practice of attention to what may lie ahead and how we may stay true to the task of building God's kingdom: Well, that's just good sense.

The prayer ends with the acknowledgement that whatever we do, whatever we may think we are, we are a part of something bigger, part of the mystery that is God. The energy we gained was pulled from that higher power, from the world around us. We are nurtured with plants grown by the power of the sun, the grace of rain, and the care of the animals that keep the soil rich. We cannot, in fairness, take sole credit. For thine is the power, the glory. And, frankly, sharing the credit is much more satisfying. Instead of pressure to perform, there is a joy and energy of a potential kingdom, even if it is just experienced in moments from time to time. But a kingdom.

Amen.

Do Unto Others

Luke 6:31-36
And as ye would that men should do to you, do ye also to them likewise. For if you love them, which love you, what thanks have ye? For sinners also love those that love them. And if you do good to them, which do good to you, what thanks have ye? For sinners also do even the same. And if you lend to them of whom you hope to receive, what thank have ye? For sinners also lend to sinners, to receive as much again. But love your enemies, and do good, and lend, hoping for nothing again; and your reward shall be great, and you shall be the children of the Highest: for he is kind unto the unthankful and to the evil. Be ye therefore merciful, as your Father also is merciful.

As ye would that men should do to you, do ye also to them likewise. Hmmm. What do I want from others? That's the first question.

My cell phone just rang. As I sat in the coffee shop, I answered it. My boss was confirming that a meeting at 12:30 today was still on. I was expecting the call and didn't even consider those around me when I answered the call. As I began to talk (a little too loudly to counter the calypso music), I became suddenly aware of the person sitting at the next table quietly focused on his computer. I made the conversation short and apologized to my neighbor. He smiled appreciatively and noted that technology has created a need for a whole new realm of etiquette that has not yet really developed. We laughed and went back to our coffee and computers. Now there is a man sitting at the table on the other side of me talking quietly on his cell phone. He is very polite. But that isn't always the way it is. Yesterday in the grocery store a young woman was standing in the chip aisle talking to her family about what to buy. Her attention was not in the store at all and I felt completely invisible as I tried (with difficulty) to pass her without disturbing her. I don't know what she expected me to do.

Today a friend of mine told me that she had trimmed her Facebook friend list. She has very good, very personal reasons for doing so; those she trimmed did nothing wrong. She just needed a break from the onslaught of messages. But she was completely unsure of the etiquette required. Did they know they had been cut? Was an explanation necessary?

We live in a world where there is a whole range of environments to consider. Cell phones, email, You Tube, Facebook, Twitter (and probably something new by the time I finish writing this.) All things that did not exist when I was growing up. Our different circumstances and personalities result in a wide range of ideas about how these tools should be used; for one an "onslaught," for another "great fun," and for yet another "business as usual."

Even coffee shops have changed. When I was growing up a coffee shop was a small restaurant with little ambiance, cinnamon rolls under glass on the counter, a waitress with a coffee pot (just one variety), a menu that included meatloaf and a BLT, and local customers who all knew each other by name. Now a coffee shop serves coffee, latte, cappuccino, and espresso, hot or iced, flavored or not, with or without foam, along with a few delectable sweets. But sitting in this particular coffee shop with me are college students working on homework, middle age friends, a woman interviewing someone for a potential consulting job, a man who looks to be in his 70s reading the paper, and one 55-year-old woman writing on her computer. No one speaks to those at the next table, though some of us come here every week. It's a different world. And somehow, we learn to adjust.

How do we treat each other in this new world? Does the woman with cartoon tattoos on her leg and bright orange hair want the same things I want? How about the old woman in the lace shirt and reading glasses who won't give up her 4-person table? Or the tourist who just wants a glass of water? Can we possibly understand each other? Who, in this bustling, anonymous community, is my enemy? Perhaps it is the person standing in the chip aisle who doesn't know I exist. Perhaps it is the person at the next table in the coffee shop. Whatever I do for these people, I certainly cannot expect any reciprocation. I may never see them again.

So, back to the first question. How do I want to be treated? I don't think it is possible for us to understand each other. We don't even know each other. But I know that I want to be treated with respect. And that means that I need to treat others with respect. The person in the chip aisle who doesn't know I exist. The person sitting next to me in the coffee shop who is still talking on his cell phone. The woman in lace who has left with a scowl. All those who understand Facebook and Twitter. All those who don't own a cell phone or a computer. Those with tattoos and orange hair. Those who are unreasonable. Those who are angry. Just respect that they are doing the best they can to manage in this complicated world; getting through another day. And I think that respect is a form of mercy.

Do You Want to be Well?

John 5:2-9
Now in Jerusalem by the Sheep Gate there is a pool which has five porticoes. In these lay many invalids – blind, lame, and paralyzed. One man was there who had been ill for 38 years. When Jesus saw him lying there and knew that he had been there a long time, he said to him, "Do you want to be made well?" The sick man answered him, "Sir, I have no one to put me into the pool when the water is stirred up; and while I am making my way, someone else steps down ahead of me." Jesus said to him, "Stand up, take your mat and walk." At once the man was made well, and he took up his mat and began to walk.

"Do you want to be made well?" What a question! Of course we all want to be made well. Don't we? But that was the first thing Jesus asked. "Do you want to be made well?" Perhaps Jesus realized that this man had been sick for a long time, had gotten used to this life of sitting with others like him by this pool. Perhaps his friends were here, also sick. What would happen if he were suddenly well? What would he talk about? Who would he talk to? Did he have a home, a job, family, friends? He had been sick for 38 years. The world had changed since he had been well. What would he face if he were made well? In fact, as soon as he got well, there was a fuss about whether it was legal for him to actually pick up his bed on the Sabbath. Life was simpler next to the pool, unable to break any laws, unable to get into trouble. Jesus asks, "Do you want to be made well?" Are you willing to face the world without excuses? Are you ready to take responsibility for your own life? It's actually a really tough question.

If you notice, the man didn't really answer the question. He told Jesus that he had been trying to get well for many years. Jesus took that as a positive answer. Yes, it appeared the man did want to be well. And that made it possible for Jesus to help him.

What Jesus did next was very simple. He so believed that the man could walk that he told him to do it. He didn't say, "Have you tried walking?" or "I'm pretty sure you could walk if you tried." He said "Stand up, take your mat and walk." That's pretty positive encouragement. What could we do if we truly believed we could?

Do you want to be made well?

Seeds

Luke 8:5-15

"A sower went out to sow his seed. And as he sowed, some fell by the way side; and it was trodden down, and the fowls of the air devoured it. And some fell upon a rock; and as soon as it was sprung up, it withered away, because it lacked moisture. And some fell among thorns; and the thorns sprang up with it, and choked it. And others fell on good ground, and sprang up, and bare fruit a hundredfold." And when he had said these things, he cried, "He that hath ears to hear, let him hear." And his disciples asked him, saying, "What might this parable be?" And he said, "Unto you it is given to know the mysteries of the kingdom of God: but to others in parables; that seeing they might not understand. Now the parable is this: The seed is the word of God. Those by the way side are they that hear; then cometh the devil, and taketh away the word out of their hearts, lest they should believe and be saved. They on the rock are they, which, when they hear, receive the word with joy; and these have no root, which for a while believe, and in time of temptation fall away. And that which fell among thorns are they, which, when they have heard, go forth and are choked with cares and riches and pleasures of this life, and bring no fruit to perfection. But that on the good ground are they, which in an honest and good heart, having heard the word, keep it, and bring forth fruit with patience."

Bring forth fruit with patience.
That's really the key, isn't it?

Patience.

The father of a two-year-old said to me one day that he thought it was entirely likely that his son would grow up to be a delinquent. The same father, when the boy was four, saw a better future for his son.

Patience.

I expect that when this boy is six, his father will believe him to be a future scientist. And through his teen years, the outlook may be very bleak.

Patience.

There are seeds in me.

Seeds of wisdom sown by professors
Explaining to me the wonders of this world and showing me how to explore beyond the classroom.

Seeds of encouragement sown by my parents
Reminding me that mistakes can be mended, sometimes completely fixed, but always learned from.

Seeds of enlightenment sown by my church
Pointing me in the way of love, justice, and forgiveness even as we struggle through religious differences and church politics.

Seeds of support sown by my friends
Believing in me when my ego has been squashed and I feel choked by thorns of an unfair and demanding world.

Seeds of beauty sown by poets and authors
Guiding me through lives different from my own; letting me glimpse the world beyond myself to teach me empathy, tolerance, and understanding.

Seeds of song sown by musicians
Pulling at my heartstrings; bringing my feelings to the surface so I can experience life more honestly and fully.

There are seeds galore!
Inside me.

Waiting.
Patiently.
Is this good ground?
Or is it full of thorns?
Rocky?
Yes. Yes. Yes.
It is all of those.

Rocky days when, I swear, any distraction pulls me away from those good seeds. The encouragement, the support, and wisdom, and they are all forgotten, replaced by the stress of today's busy world.

Thorny days when it feels like all the elements have conspired against me. The beauty is overshadowed by fear and despair.

Remember patience.

On good days, I remember the seeds sown.
I let those roots grow; knowing it may take some time.
I tend to each seed with the attention it deserves.

Patience.

And slowly
In my tenuous soul
The seeds grow.

Good Neighbors

Luke 10:25-37
And behold, a certain lawyer stood up, and tempted Jesus, saying, "Master, what shall I do to inherit eternal life?" He said unto him, "What is written in the law? How readest thou?" And he answering said, "Thou shalt love the Lord thy God with all thy heart, and with all thy soul, and with all thy strength, and with all thy mind; and thy neighbor as thyself." And he said unto him, "Thou hast answered right. This do, and thou shalt live." But he, willing to justify himself, said unto Jesus, "And who is my neighbor?" And Jesus answering said, "A certain man went down from Jerusalem to Jericho and fell among thieves, which stripped him of his raiment and wounded him, and departed, leaving him half dead. And by chance there came down a certain priest that way and when he saw him, he passed by on the other side. And likewise a Levite, when he was at the place, came and looked on him, and passed by on the other side. But a certain Samaritan, as he journeyed, came where he was: and when he saw him, he had compassion on him. And went to him, and bound up his wounds, pouring in oil and wine, and set him on his own beast, and brought him to an inn, and took care of him. And on the morrow when he departed, he took out two pence, and gave them to the host, and said unto him, 'Take care of him; and whatsoever thou spendest more, when I come again, I will repay thee.' Which now of these three, thinkest thou, was neighbor unto him that fell among the thieves?" And he said, "He that showed mercy on him." Then said Jesus unto him, "Go, and do thou likewise."

The obvious response to the famous Good Samaritan story is to feel responsible for helping out. What can I possibly say that would be new or insightful? Of course we need to help out. And God knows there are a host of opportunities. But I have to admit that I can relate to the lawyer who asks, "Who is my neighbor?" – hoping to narrow those opportunities down a bit. I want to say, "I helped my mom with her taxes. And I cheered up a friend and showed my sister some cool things on her computer. I took my grandson to the beach. Those count, don't they? And besides, if I saw someone in REAL trouble, I'd stop. I really would. If I could." But I know that I really don't want to disrupt my life too much.

I open the occasional door for a handicapped person (but only if I'm close by). I give money to the homeless shelter (if it's in my budget.) I give donations to Goodwill (things I don't want any more). I'm a good person, if it's convenient.

I try to think of the times in my life I really reached out, really went out of my way to help someone I didn't already care about. I have to go back a ways. I was in high school and a family in our church was struggling. The father had a teaching job, but his salary just barely covered the expenses generated by four children. They managed to scrape by, but there was no money for anything extra. At Christmas, my mom, sister, and I shopped for luscious fabric and sewed pretty dresses for the girls. We made toys for the smaller children. It was a time-intensive project and not without costs. We wrapped the gifts and snuck in on Christmas Eve to deliver the gifts. We saw a need and knew we had the means to help.

During my high school years, I also made stuffed animals for kids in the local hospital. I volunteered at the same hospital on Christmas and Thanksgiving so that those who remained bed-ridden over these special days would not be alone. I realize that my parents were very good neighbors and made it seem easy and fun to join in.

In college I was a camp counselor, accepting the challenge of the cabin of girls considered "difficult." And upon graduating from college, I headed up a crew for the annual Paint-A-Thon in Minnesota's Twin Cities, painting the home of someone without the means to get it done themselves. It was a grueling day or two of work.

But somewhere along the way, I stopped doing these things. Perhaps it started with the increasing need for two-income households. As I took on more responsibility at work, I worked longer hours and came home exhausted, content to watch TV. My own health issues, a disintegrating marriage, and a cross-country move further drained my resources of time and money. Assisting aging parents, helping graduating children move on, babysitting grandchildren and trying to be a good boss has taken my energy, a commodity considerably less abundant as I grow older. I tell myself the things I'm doing are important, and I think they are.

But I also miss the joy I felt as I looked at the faces of my stuffed critters and hugged each one before I sent them off to the hospital. I miss the excitement I felt at the prospect of giving just one family an unexpectedly merry Christmas. I miss the camaraderie of the painting team; none of us particularly interested in house painting, but willing to give it a try. And I remember that I always felt blessed that I could help make the world a little better place. Being a neighbor had its benefits, for both the receiver and the giver.

I think helping family does count. I really do. But I think I need to reach out a little further, at least once in a while. After all, the Good Samaritan didn't actually go that far out of his way. But when he encountered a need in his path, he stopped and did what he could. I think I just need to be a little more aware of neighbor opportunities that are in my daily path. As opportunities arise, I will try to use a little of my time and energy to be a good neighbor. And thinking of this potential makes me smile.

Life is Good

John 8:12
I am the light of the world; he that followeth me shall not walk in darkness, but shall have the light of life.

My dad died last week. It was not unexpected. He was 80. He had been sick for a long time. Cancer. Slow deterioration over four years. Then a sudden rapid decline over three days. And then he was gone. I sat next to him the day he died; told him how much I loved him. We celebrated his life at his memorial service. Dad had lived life to the fullest. He traveled the world, lived his values at work, served his church, volunteered untiringly, shared his wealth, loved his family, and laughed every day. Dad saw the light of this world. He did not walk in darkness. Clear up until the week he died his favorite saying was, "Life is good."

I have not been so sure. I struggle with depression; I let the difficulties of life get me down. Too often I walk in darkness, engulfed by the shadows that inevitably accompany life, failing to see the light that is always present beyond those shadows.

I'm not sure why Dad was so convinced that life was good. He had been born during the Great Depression, wearing only hand-me-downs and mismatched shoes most of his childhood. Mental illness plagued his family and brought challenges from many fronts throughout his life. His own congenital eye disease made many areas of life difficult. And of course, there was the cancer. But Dad was determined to walk in the light, and these "shadows" simply did not pull him down.

We put a picture of Dad in front of the hall where we held his memorial. He was healthy and smiling, the way I like to remember him. When I looked at the picture, it made me smile, even as we were recovering from the horror of his last few days on earth. Dad looked happy to be here; guiding those who looked to him into the light of the world; wanting them to enjoy the good life he had so recently left behind.

I think God must have loved the world to give us Dad. Dad didn't ask others to follow him. But he did proclaim to all that would listen that life was good. His love for life was contagious. Those who met him did not walk in darkness. And those who keep his smile in their hearts will walk in light.

Making Plans

Matthew 6:26-33
"Behold the fowls of the air; for they sow not, neither do they reap, nor gather into barns; yet your heavenly father feedeth them. Are ye not much better than they? Which of you by taking thought can add one cubit unto his stature? And why take you thought for raiment? Consider the lilies of the field, how they grow; they toil not, neither do they spin: And yet I say unto you, That even Solomon in all his glory was not arrayed like one of these. Wherefore, if God so clothe the grass of the field, which today is, and tomorrow is cast into the oven, shall he not much more clothe you, O ye of little faith? Therefore take no thought of saying, 'What shall we eat?' Or 'What shall we drink?' Or, 'Wherewithal shall we be clothed?' ...For your heavenly Father knoweth that ye have need of all these things. But seek ye first the kingdom of God, and his righteousness; and all these things shall be added unto you."

I spent yesterday planning for tomorrow. I rented a truck to help move my stepson to his own apartment. I talked to my financial planner to allocate my retirement funds so that I will (hopefully) have money when I retire. I joined Weight Watchers in hopes of losing the weight my doctor feels I need to lose. I made appointments to get a doctor's checkup and take my car in for a tune-up. I am planning for my svelte, healthy, child free, self-sufficient retirement, coming up all to quickly. When I get there, I will be set! And happy! I hope...

Yesterday's breakfast was the usual: raisin toast, banana, and iced Chai. No thought required. Lunch was a frozen entrée, straight out of the fridge. No thought there, either. Dinner was in front of the TV. I can't remember what I ate or if my cat sat on my lap. I didn't call Mom. I was busy planning my future.

By the end of the day I was tired and grumpy. And I wondered why. I'd have to bring this up with my therapist.

But not all days are like this. Some days I savor each bite of my usual breakfast – I really like bananas - and I feel energized. Some days I celebrate the sun or the rain outside and feel eager to face the world. Some days I notice creation, the fowls of the air and the lilies of the field, and it fills me with an appreciation and calm that helps me face a crazy world with loving-kindness. On those days, I call Mom to check in and make sure she is OK. And in turn she makes me smile with some bit of wisdom or a funny story of her adventures. Some days I actively see and experience this kingdom of God, all around me. And it lifts me up. Thoughts of chocolate disappear as I sit listening to the sound of waves. I can go help my stepson move with a cheerful heart, able to celebrate and support his new independence. When I seek out images of the holy, I find them everywhere – in dancing children, a couple holding hands, a colorful painting, the smell of coffee. Maybe that doesn't help my stock portfolio. Or maybe it does. Good energy is contagious. How would a world of energized, beauty-seeking people affect the stock market? I don't think it would hurt.

I will have another planning day, probably next week. I have to update my website, buy groceries, and plan a vacation (God knows I need one.) But perhaps on that day, I should seek FIRST the kingdom of God around me: Savor my breakfast, find bunnies in the clouds, notice the dancing children and my purring cat. Call Mom. And then, using the energy that God's creation has for me, move ahead with my plans.

Brokenness

Matthew 8:5-13
And when Jesus was entered into Capernaum, there came unto him a centurion, beseeching him, and saying, "Lord, my servant lieth at home sick of the palsy, grievously tormented." And Jesus saith unto him, "I will come and heal him." The centurion answered and said, "Lord, I am not worthy that thou shouldest come under my roof. But speak the word only, and my servant shall be healed. For I am a man under authority, having soldiers under me. And I say to this man, 'Go,' and he goeth; and to another, 'Come' and he cometh; and to my servant, 'Do this,' and he doeth it." When Jesus heard it, he marveled and said to them that followed, "Verily I say unto you, I have not found so great faith, no, not in Israel. And I say unto you, that many shall come from the east and west, and shall sit down with Abraham, and Isaac, and Jacob, in the kingdom of heaven. But the children of the kingdom shall be cast out into outer darkness: there shall be weeping and gnashing of teeth." And Jesus said unto the centurion, "Go thy way; and as thou hast believed, so be it done unto thee." And his servant was healed in the selfsame hour.

We are broken.
Every one of us.

None of us escapes without some cracks early on. Life is a risky venture. We are fragile beings left in the custody of the untrained with inadequate resources. We get scratched even in the best of situations. And most of us sustain some pretty severe injuries. The miracle is that we survive at all. But we do. Initially we don't recognize our brokenness. As we grow, we learn how to handle ourselves in a way that our wounds don't show too much. Sometimes we deny our weaknesses altogether. But we are all broken.

We need healing.
Every one of us.

But to ask is just too hard. It would require an admission of weakness. Those wounds we've been hiding would be exposed. And what could anyone really do? After all, they are broken, too. And, truth be known, we aren't actually worthy of such a gift.
But we all need healing.

What if we asked for healing?
Every one of us.

That might be enough.
To open up the wound to the air might be enough to relieve the pain. If we relaxed those muscles that we use to hide the flaws, if we just accepted ourselves as broken, looked at the beauty that is left instead of using our energy to hide.
It might be enough
To ask for a healing.

And what if just one person who saw our wounds truly believed that we could be healed?
Just one of them.

Believed that we were worthy of such a healing.
Believed that they could help.
Perhaps we would find that those who care about us already knew of our broken places; are ready for our call should it come. Could we let those who care about us, those who believe we can be healed, help us? That just might be enough to actually mend the cracks and scratches.
If just one believed.

And what if you were the one who saw the wound?
Would you recognize the need?
Would you believe enough that healing is possible?
Knowing that you yourself are broken and in need of healing?
Or would you hide inside your patched and bandaged shell,
Waiting for someone else to heal you?
Feeling unworthy to heal or be healed.

We are all broken.
Every one of us.

Forgiving Sins

Matthew 9:1-8
And Jesus came into his own city. And behold, they brought to him a man sick of the palsy, lying on a bed: and Jesus seeing their faith said unto the sick of the palsy, "Son, be of good cheer; thy sins be forgiven thee." And behold, certain of the scribes said within themselves, "This man blasphemeth." And Jesus knowing their thoughts said, "Wherefore think ye evil in your hearts? For whether is easier, to say, 'Thy sins be forgiven thee,' or to say, 'Arise, and walk?' But that ye may know that the Son of man hath power on earth to forgive sins." Then said he to the sick of the palsy, "Arise, take up thy bed, and go unto thine house."

A woman I know struggles with a mental illness that leaves her terrified of being less than perfect. Any imperfection, she feels, will make her unworthy of love. She "reads between the lines" and discovers disapproval in all that is said to her. She spends much of her time and energy trying to justify her behavior, hiding mistakes, or blaming others for problems. She is fearful, anxious, often contentious, and very lonely. Daily she struggles to keep those she loves close, often with very counter-productive tactics.

Hers is an extreme case, but I think perhaps we are all just a little afraid of disapproval.

Although the disorder in the man brought to Jesus was palsy, Jesus saw beyond the exterior. He recognized the fear and longing inside the human heart and granted forgiveness. He knew the man would not ask for forgiveness. And he knew that perhaps the sickness in the man was, at least in part, due to a heaviness of heart. A man who knows he had made mistakes but is unable to admit them does not expect forgiveness. But Jesus didn't wait to be asked. The scribes did not even believe Jesus had the power to forgive sins. But Jesus didn't consider who had the power. He saw a need and granted forgiveness.

What would we do if, when we asked for help, the person pronounced that our sins were forgiven? Would we defend our honor and say we had nothing to be forgiven of? Would we turn our nose up, saying that no one has the power to forgive our sins? Or would we rejoice, that someone knew our sins and still loved us enough to forgive us our indiscretions? That, in spite of being imperfect, we were worthy of love? Perhaps forgiveness would be harder for us to accept than a healing.

And what if we saw someone else in pain? Would we be able to look into their heart and see the longing for affection, for forgiveness? Could we grant forgiveness, even silently (so as not to hurt their pride)? And would forgiving them, make it easier for us to help them? Perhaps forgiveness would be harder to give than a physical blessing. But perhaps we should try.

Rich Toward God

Luke 12:16-21
And Jesus told a parable unto them, saying, The ground of a certain rich man brought forth plentifully: And he thought within himself, saying, "What shall I do, because I have no room where to bestow my fruits?" And he said, "This will I do: I will pull down my barns, and build greater; and there will I bestow all my fruits and my goods. And I will say to my soul, 'Soul, thou hast much goods laid up for many years; take thine ease, eat, drink, and be merry.'" But God said unto him, "Thou fool, this night thy soul shall be required of thee: then whose shall those things be which thou hast provided?" So is he that layeth up treasure for himself, and is not rich toward God.

It is fall. Squirrels are burying nuts. Bears, fat from the summer fruits, are starting to think about their yearly hibernation. The days are shorter (less time for activity) and the nights are longer, a suggestion that perhaps we need more rest. My aunt spent the fall canning the garden harvest. Putting the summer in jars for the winter. Laying up goods for the future.

But I have Safeway and Trader Joe's. I let them do the canning and preserving. I don't have much space in my apartment for storing up things for winter, much less for many years. So I guess I'm not guilty of laying up treasure for myself. No room. No plans for bigger barns.

But this is a parable, so I'm going to have to look beyond the literal. What am I storing? Well, there are retirement funds. I have no children to take care of me when I get old, so it is important for me to save up something. But perhaps that's not the meaning either. Think. What am I storing?

Books. I have tons of books. Thank goodness for floor-to-ceiling bookcases. Videos, DVDs, and music. Lots of music. Artwork (mostly images of trees I have created and stored away, hoping to sell when I get around to having another show). Rocks. Rocks from every trip to every beach I've ever visited. Photos, memories of good times, people long gone. Fortunately digital technology lets me keep them all, and I do. I have a small, but precious, collection of friends and family. And I have to admit to doing a little storing up of time and energy for myself.

So, I have my own unique set of treasures. But the sin is not in storing, but in storing for myself AND not being rich toward God. What does that mean? Rich toward God. I looked this up in several translations and kept finding the same word. "Toward." A word that conveys a direction, recognition, and possibly movement.

To be rich toward God seems to require some recognition of where God is.
To be rich toward God seems to require some recognition of my own value, my own riches.
This is hard for me.
But "hard" is not "impossible." "Hard" is a challenge that usually results in growth. But "hard" is still hard.

So, with my retirement funds, my books, my music, my rocks and photos and precious people, I look for God. And surprisingly, I find God in my books, music, rocks, photos, and friends. Maybe I am part of someone else's stored up riches. Maybe I am part of God's treasure.

Rich toward God. Rich toward music, toward friends, toward rocks and trees.

Facing these things; these pieces of the divine, I search my soul for what comes next. I think recognition is the first step: to see each person, book, concerto, animal, tree, snowflake and rock as a vessel for God; to face them with recognition of their value to me and to the world. To be rich toward God indicates a direction, but not necessarily movement. Perhaps recognition, a mindset, is what is required. A mindset that treasure is not stored, but appreciated and shared. I think that would change the way we treat others, the things we choose to do. And movement toward a more gracious world, toward God, would be inevitable.

Worth Saving

Luke 15:11-32
A certain man had two sons: And the younger of them said to his father, "Father, give me the portion of goods that falleth to me." And he divided unto them his living. And not many days after the younger son gathered all together, and took his journey into a far country, and there wasted his substance with riotous living. And when he had spent all, there arose a mighty famine in that land; and he began to be in want. And he went and joined himself to a citizen of that country; and he sent him into his fields to feed swine. And he would fain have filled his belly with the husks that the swine did eat: and no man gave unto him. And when he came to himself, he said, "How many hired servants of my father's have bread enough and to spare, and I perish with hunger! I will arise and go to my father, and will say unto him, 'Father, I have sinned against heaven, and before thee, And am no more worthy to be called thy son: make me as one of thy hired servants.'" And he arose, and came to his father. But when he was yet a great way off, his father saw him, and had compassion, and ran, and fell on his neck, and kissed him. And the son said unto him, "Father, I have sinned against heaven, and in thy sight, and am no more worthy to be called thy son." But the father said to his servants, "Bring forth the best robe, and put it on him; and put a ring on his hand, and shoes on his feet: And bring hither the fatted calf, and kill it; and let us eat and be merry: For this my son was dead and is alive again; he was lost and is found." And they began to be merry. Now his elder son was in the field: and as he came and drew nigh to the house, he heard music and dancing. And he called one of the servants and asked what these things meant. And he said unto him, "Thy brother is come; and thy father hath killed the fatted calf, because he hath received him safe and sound." And he was angry, and would not go in: therefore came his father out, and entreated him. And he answering said to his father, "Lo, these many years do I serve thee, neither transgressed I at any time thy commandment: and yet thou never gavest me a kid, that I might make merry with my friends: But as soon as this thy son was come, which hath devoured thy living with harlots, thou hast killed for him the fatted calf." And he said unto him, "Son, thou art ever with me, and all that I have is thine. It was meet that we should make merry, and be glad: for this thy brother was dead, and is alive again; and was lost, and is found."

I normally relate to the older son in the story of the Prodigal Son. I have played the part of the good kid. Life most families, mine had its share of difficulties. So, it was my job to not cause a stir. I made good grades. I was in by curfew. I cleaned my room and never asked for money. I was an active participating church member. The fact that I was something of a geek in high school made this fairly easy. I went to college at my parents' alma mater, a small church college in rural Iowa. There were limited avenues for misadventure. And although I did find a few of them, I managed to remain in generally good graces with my parents. I, like the older son, sometimes felt irritated that so much of my parents' efforts went into managing other family issues. I was often left to my own devices. They knew I'd be OK. I always was.

Then I met Ted. I was in college with a stellar grade point and great career prospects. Ted was the son of a missionary. His hair was too long. He was a vegetarian (which in the "heart of cattle country" in the mid 1970s was pretty odd) and a passionate defender of animal rights. He played in a rock band. He thought monogamy was out-dated. He drove a rusted out 1940 Plymouth that he could not afford to maintain. He was everything I was not: rebellious, unconventional and cool. Eager for new experiences, I became a vegetarian and refused to wear leather. I stopped going to church, argued against the status quo and even skipped classes. I bought new tires for his vintage car and helped pay for gas (which it guzzled.) And I fell out of good graces with just about everyone, including my teachers, my roommate, and my parents. "They don't understand," I protested, thinking that they were just not enlightened. I didn't go home for Christmas. Instead, I accompanied Ted to see his family. To my parents, I may not have been dead, but I was certainly lost.

After a while, the smokescreen of "cool" began to settle. I realized that Ted, though not a bad person, really was not right for me. Since he was also seeing other girls, I sat home alone on Valentine's Day. I got the first C of my entire academic career, and it was in my major. I became anemic and landed in the hospital. My roommate moved out. My parents were silent. My math professor was disappointed. And soon the cool boyfriend was gone, too. I had to reevaluate.

I was lucky that my best friend never abandoned me and provided a friendly place to admit my sins. As I dumped my sorrows, I knew I had hurt some of the people most precious to me. And I had hurt myself. I felt lost. So, I was no longer the good kid. And, like the prodigal son, I returned to my roots. I went back to church and found community and spiritual strength. I hit the books, even pursuing a Masters degree that has served me well in my career. And I asked forgiveness of my parents. Fortunately, they ran to meet me, arms open, willing to celebrate my return. And I was glad that this time, when I became the "difficulty", when I needed their attention, they let the others in their lives fend for themselves.

I didn't come out of the situation unchanged. I eat less meat than I did before. I still think rock bands are cool, though I never reprised the role of "groupie." I admire, but avoid owning, old cars. And I still love long hair on men.

From time to time, Mom recalls the year of Ted, the lost year. We laugh, glad it is over. Somehow with the clarity of hindsight, it seems inevitable and natural that Ted and I would split and I would return home. But at the time, it wasn't that clear. I recall that it was hard to return. Very hard. I wasn't willing to completely admit that I had strayed. I blamed Ted for abandoning me. Since Mom and Dad didn't like him, we could all bond in our mutual anger at Ted. It was a start. It took me more time to admit that I had not been entirely fair to others during this time. I expect it was hard for Mom and Dad, too. They wanted their daughter back. But the daughter that they found was a changed daughter. A wiser one. A daughter who recognized the importance of family and friends and would work to preserve those relationships. But a daughter who had learned that she did not, could not, follow completely in her parents' footsteps. She was her own person. She had moved from being the compliant child to being an adult handling the delicate balance of self-actualization and precious relationships. And fortunately, my parents recognized that this was worthy of celebration.

It would be nice if I could say that from that point forward, I never strayed far from the good graces of my parents. But that would be a lie. I have had lapses over the years when I didn't handle that balance very well. In my desire to explore some new path, I hurt someone's feelings. Whether from insensitivity, anger or stupidity, I paid the price. But I continue to realize the value of friends and family, ministers and teachers. And so I return a little wiser, asking forgiveness. And each time they find the grace to forgive me and accept me back.

I am indebted to my parents and to all those who have been willing to keep watch when I am lost and accept me when I'm willing to be found. I hope I can be as gracious to others.

Rich or Poor

Luke 16:19-31
There was a certain rich man, who was clothed in purple and fine linen, and fared sumptuously every day: And there was a certain beggar named Lazarus, who was laid at his gate, full of sores, and desiring to be fed with the crumbs which fell from the rich man's table. Moreover, the dogs came and licked his sores. And it came to pass that the beggar died and was carried by the angels into Abraham's bosom. The rich man also died, and was buried. And in hell he lifted up his eyes, being in torments, and saw Abraham afar off, and Lazarus in his bosom. And he cried and said, "Father Abraham, have mercy on me, and send Lazarus, that he may dip the tip of his finger in water and cool my tongue, for I am tormented in this flame." But Abraham said, "Son, remember that thou in thy lifetime received thy good things, and likewise Lazarus evil things: but now he is comforted, and thou art tormented. And beside all this, between us and you there is a great gulf fixed: so that they, who would pass from hence to you, cannot; neither can they pass to us that would come from thence." Then he said, "I pray thee therefore, father, that thou wouldst send him to my father's house. For I have five brethren; that he may testify unto them, lest they also come into this place of torment." Abraham said unto him, "They have Moses and the prophets. Let them hear them." And he said, "Nay, father Abraham. But if one went unto them from the dead, they will repent." And he said unto him, "If they hear not Moses and the prophets, neither will they be persuaded, though one rose from the dead."

Some days I am the rich man;
Not with millions, but fashionable.
Going to the theater;
Eating good food; warm.
Walking by the homeless who ask to eat my crumbs
Without looking.

Some days I am the beggar;
Not penniless, but feeling lonely.
Unable to cope on my own;
Struggling with life; cold.
Looking to those who seem rich with strength and love
To help me.

Why is it that I swing to such extremes?
Ah, but perhaps they are closer than I realize.
The rich too afraid of losing her possessions
To give anything away.
The beggar too afraid of losing her soul
To show strength.

What will become of me?
Will I be offered healing waters?
Or tormented with fire?
Perhaps both.

What will I do now?
Who am I listening to?
Who guides my actions?
Too many voices.

But today I will listen to the prophets.
Today I will work toward awareness.
I will recognize the riches I posses.
The love of my family and friends.

Good food to eat,
A warm bed,
Good shoes,
An occasional latte.
I will be the rich man, with love and strength
Enough to share.

Today I will work toward balance.
Knowing that within my limited means,
There is always something I can give;
Love,
Encouragement,
Laughter,
An occasional meal.
I will remember that I have been a beggar
And will be again.
Hoping to find a rich man who listens to the prophets.

Return Rate

Luke 17:12-19
And as he entered into a certain village, there met him ten men that were lepers, which stood afar off: And they lifted up their voices, and said, Jesus, Master, have mercy on us. And when he saw them, he said unto them, "Go show yourselves unto the priests." And it came to pass, that, as they went, they were cleansed. And one of them, when he saw that he was healed, turned back, and with a loud voice glorified God, And fell down on his face at his feet, giving him thanks: and he was a Samaritan. And Jesus answering said," Were there not ten cleansed? But where are the nine? There are not found that returned to give glory to God, save this stranger." And he said unto him, "Arise, go thy way: thy faith hath made thee whole."

I have some difficult people in my life;
People who seem to sap the energy from me.
"I am suffering and no one else will help me."
So I help.
And off they go, unaware that I need something from them.
At least I WANT something from them.
"Thank you."
"You are such a good person."
That's all.
Just a good word, to boost my self-esteem.
No cost in that. Just words.
Credit for my good works.
Is that so much to ask?
Even Jesus wanted acknowledgement.
He healed the lepers. That's a pretty darn good deed.
And nine of the ten didn't say "thanks."
Ninety percent.
And yet Jesus kept on healing, doing good work.
I'm not always so charitable.
"I'm not helping her any more. She doesn't appreciate it."

"Why give money? They just misuse it."
If my effort isn't appreciated,
If my money isn't used the way I think it should,
If I don't get anything out of it,
I want to quit.
Give up.
Put my efforts into something a little more satisfying.
But Jesus kept on doing good work.
Aware that his "return rate" would likely be only 10 percent.
He had a sense of who he was,
What he was about in this world,
That was not dependent on the acknowledgement of others.
What if Jesus had decided how to act based on what he would get in return?

I need to decide who I am going to be in this world
What I will do and how I will act
What I will contribute.
And if 10% of the time I get a heartfelt "thank you",
I'm doing pretty darn good.

Who am I?

Luke 18:10-14
Two men went up into the temple to pray; the one a Pharisee, and the other a publican. The Pharisee stood and prayed thus with himself, God, I thank thee, that I am not as other men are, extortioners, unjust, adulterers, or even as this publican. I fast twice in the week; I give tithes of all that I possess. And the publican, standing afar off, would not lift up so much as his eyes unto heaven, but smote upon his breast, saying, God be merciful to me a sinner. I tell you, this man went down to his house justified rather than the other: for every one that exalteth himself shall be abased; and he that humbleth himself shall be exhalted.

My friend, Jennifer Ryu, preached a sermon the day before Martin Luther King Day. The sermon revolved around a 1960s sit-in staged by four black students at a Woolworth lunch counter in Alabama. She showed us a photo of the black students as well as a couple of white patrons sitting at the counter with security and onlookers nearby. She asked us to think about who we identified with in the picture. Then she related testimony of the various people involved that day.

There were the unwelcome "colored" students who decided to make a stand by sitting where they were not allowed. Although I cannot claim to fully understand what it is like to be the brunt of racial inequity, I have experienced injustice simply because I am female. I know the mixed feelings of anger, frustration, resoluteness, piety, and fear that go into making a stand. I have stood firm for the right of women to be treated equally. Yes, I consider myself a righteous protector of justice.

There were the white friends who were told they were welcome to stay. I have been in this position. At a bowling alley in Fort Dodge Iowa back in the mid-1970s, we were told in no uncertain terms that three of us could bowl, but they would not sell shoes to our black friend. He had his own shoes, so we stayed only to have our recreation tainted by loud and unkind remarks. Unwilling to fight the battle that day, we all agreed to find more friendly territory. So I have had a taste of being on the side of right. But I have to question whether I have the ability to really hold on in tough times. Maybe I was just a supporter of justice, not really a righteous protector.

At the lunch counter there was a woman who just happened to be there, finishing her meal as the confrontation began. She hurriedly finished and left, telling a reporter that while she supported racial justice, her family simply would not understand. She had to get home. I hate to admit that I can understand this view, too. How many times had I avoided a difficult discussion because it might jeopardize my relationship? I didn't side with prejudice, but I didn't counter it either. I kept my mouth shut and hoped my silence would make my disagreement known. Maybe I'm just a person who hopes for justice.

I like to think I am a good person. I try to be. I really do. And there are days that I boost myself up, patting myself on the back for taking the side of the right, for not being like those who are racist, apathetic, or weak. And I think that giving myself a little credit from time to time is OK. But when I have a good day, a day when I can stand proud of my actions, I have to remember not to be too hard on others who may seem racist, apathetic or weak. When I am honest, there are days that I am sure I must have appeared to be all those things. I have spoken insensitive words; unaware of the wounds my words have re-opened. I have tuned out the needs of the world when my busy schedule took control of my life. I have turned away when my own wounds made me unable to help others. Despite the longing in my heart to do right, I have not always chosen correctly. I have made mistakes that have hurt others. So perhaps we are all kindred souls, longing to do right, unsure of how to respond, unable to do all that is required.

God, I thank thee that I am surrounded by good role models, people who fight for justice, who care for others, who make the world a better place. I thank thee that on my best days, I am able to count myself among those brave and charitable people. And God, I admit that there are days I am not so kind. My fear of ridicule or rejection, the hurt I have experienced and subsequent anger, and my own ignorance not only keep me from doing good, but actually lead me to insensitive and hurtful actions. I am in need of forgiveness and mercy. Thank you for merciful people who can see my potential, even on my bad days, and give me the support I need to rise above my own demons.

Amen.

Sinners and Teachers

Luke 19:1-10
And Jesus entered and passed through Jericho. And, behold, there was a man named Zacchaeus, who was the chief among the publicans, and he was rich. And he sought to see Jesus who he was; and could not for the press, because he was little of stature. And he ran before, and climbed up into a sycamore tree to see him: for he was to pass that way. And when Jesus came to the place, he looked up, and saw him, and said unto him, "Zacchaeus, make haste, and come down; for today I must abide at thy house." And he made haste, and came down, and received him joyfully. And when they saw it, they all murmured, saying that he was gone to be guest with a man that is a sinner. And Zacchaeus stood, and said unto the Lord, "Behold, Lord, the half of my goods I give to the poor; and if I have taken any thing from any man by false accusation, I restore him fourfold." And Jesus said unto him, "This day is salvation come to this house, forasmuch as he also is a son of Abraham. For the Son of man is come to seek and to save that which was lost."

Who would you climb a tree to see?
The winner of the latest reality show who makes us believe
that we, too, can strike it rich and famous?
The eloquent preacher who promises healing and eternal life?
The politician who promises jobs and lower taxes?
Will any of them deliver on their promises?
Is it worth climbing the tree?

Who do the rich and famous go to see?

Zacchaeus, a rich man (and possibly famous), climbed a tree to see a teacher; One who inspired him,
A man who made him care about things other than riches or fame.
And Jesus sensed his enthusiastic search and invited himself into Zacchaeus' home, into his heart.

And the priests murmured.

It isn't right for a teacher to dine with a sinner.

I think that sometimes I am the sinner, the one others look down on, looking at my past and expecting little.
But I am still a seeker, jockeying for a spot in the crowd, looking for someone who will inspire me and give me the new direction I want, but don't know how to find on my own. As the sinner, I need to believe I can change.

Sometimes I think I may be the teacher, the one others look to for direction, seeing my past successes, expecting a lot.
I feel inadequate, uncomfortable with admiration. But I do have something to give, and I have a responsibility to invite myself into the lives of others, even those in whom people have little faith. And I need to allow them to change.

I am both the sinner and the teacher. And I am surrounded by others who are sinners and teachers. As I search for new direction, I will look around me, climb trees if I must, to find the inspiration I need to change for the better.

Walking on Water

Matthew 14:22-33
Immediately He made the disciples get into the boat and go ahead of Him to the other side, while He sent the crowds away. After He had sent the crowds away, He went up on the mountain by Himself to pray; and when it was evening, He was there alone. But the boat was already a long distance from the land, battered by the waves; for the wind was contrary. And in the fourth watch of the night He came to them, walking on the sea. When the disciples saw Him walking on the sea, they were terrified, and said, "It is a ghost!" And they cried out in fear. But immediately Jesus spoke to them, saying, "Take courage, it is I; do not be afraid." Peter said to Him, "Lord, if it is you, command me to come to you on the water." And He said, "Come!" And Peter got out of the boat, and walked on the water and came toward Jesus. But seeing the wind, he became frightened, and beginning to sink, he cried out, "Lord, save me!" Immediately Jesus stretched out His hand and took hold of him, and said to him, "You of little faith, why did you doubt?" When they got into the boat, the wind stopped. And those who were in the boat worshiped Him, saying, "You are certainly God's Son!"

Some time ago, I was loading my car for an art show. I had loaded my artwork and only had two heavy tables left to put on top of my car. I have done this by myself before and I planned to do it myself today. But when I started to do it, I found that my arms just couldn't handle it. I looked around and saw that my neighbors, a young couple, were sitting on their porch. The job of putting the tables on my car was easy with two people, so I walked over and asked if one of them might be willing to help me. The young man looked at me and said, "Tell me I have to do it." I was taken aback. "What?" I replied. Surely I had not heard him correctly. "Tell me I have to do it," he said again.

I wasn't sure what to do. I really needed the help and he was obviously capable of doing it and had not told me he wouldn't do it. But to demand his help was not something I was really comfortable doing. "I would really appreciate your help." I ventured. But he persisted. "Tell me I have to do it." I must have looked really bewildered at this point, because his wife said very matter-of-factly, "Just tell him to do it."

So, I did. "Come help me load these tables on my car." Up he jumped and cheerfully helped me with my tables.

"Lord, if it is you, command me to come to you on the water."

What is it inside us that requires a command in order to venture outside our comfort zone? My neighbor was a bit on the strange side, no doubt about that. But there is something familiar about his behavior. Sometimes the cautious child in me waits until someone else does it first. There are tasks I've avoided until my boss tells me I have to do it. I was really hoping someone else would venture into the unknown, that they would take the blame if it didn't work out. My faith does not kick in until someone makes the command, believing I can do it. And sometimes their belief is enough.

But sometimes when the task is difficult or completely new, like "walking on water," the command only gets me out of the boat. In order to actually perform this seemingly impossible task, I need more than their faith. I need my own faith. I need to believe I have what it takes to do the task at hand. And sometimes that is really, really hard.

"Save me!" I say to my boss. "Can't you do this for me?"
"Save me!" I say to my friends. "You've done this. Help me through it."
"Save me!" I wail to God. "How could you get me in this spot?"

And sometimes, they come to my rescue (and I really, really appreciate it). But, I didn't get to walk on water. I had to go back to the safety of the boat. I missed out on something really exciting. No bragging rights or great stories for the grandchildren. But safe. Still in my comfort zone. Content to say, "Who really wants to walk on water anyway?"

What if we were listening for the call instead of trying to avoid it?
What if we heard the request, not waiting for a command, and jumped at the opportunity?
What if we had faith in ourselves and in those around us to step up to the task?
What great stories we'd have for our grandchildren.

Stay and Rest

Matthew 14:14-22
Jesus saw a large crowd, and felt compassion for them and healed their sick. When it was evening, the disciples came to Him and said, "This place is desolate and the hour is already late; so send the crowds away, that they may go into the villages and buy food for themselves." But Jesus said to them, "They do not need to go away; you give them something to eat!" They said to Him, "We have here only five loaves and two fish." And He said, "Bring them here to me." Ordering the people to sit down on the grass, He took the five loaves and the two fish, and looking up toward heaven, He blessed the food, and breaking the loaves He gave them to the disciples, and the disciples gave them to the crowds, and they all ate and were satisfied. They picked up what was left over of the broken pieces, twelve full baskets. There were about five thousand men who ate, besides women and children.

I'm grumpy today. I've been working hard, both at work and at family affairs. A funeral. A move. A stolen car. A new system at work. A dead battery. Finally it's my time for fun, but I'm tired. I want to just sit and rest. I have reservations for fun in the sun by the sea. But I really just want to stay here and rest.

I would like to sit on the hillside and be fed by a compassionate healer. That would be nice. No need to run to the store, shop and cook. I can just sit here and rest. Perhaps that is why the multitude stayed there, knowing there were only five loaves and two fishes. They were tired and just wanted to rest. "Perhaps the bread will make it to me. And I have some cheese in my bag, enough to share with the people next to me. With some bread, that will be enough. And we can all stay here and rest." And as the meager loaves and fishes were passed, perhaps there was more cheese and some veggies from a garden, and a few figs to help them make it through the day. And as one shared, as he set the example of sharing his embarrassingly inadequate fare, others found that their baskets were not so meager as they thought.

Perhaps they could share a little, so that those sitting beside them could stay and rest. Perhaps there were a few in the crowd who weren't so tired and (eager to help out or to enjoy the company of a happy, peaceful crowd) scurried into town for more food; their energy allowing others to rest.

When you think about it, it's a miracle that no one scoffed at Jesus' offering. Five loaves and two fishes, no matter how big each might have been, were pitiful, really. This food was meant to feed a handful of men, not a crowd. How silly to offer it, as if it would actually satisfy the crowd. Was it arrogance or naiveté that made him do it? Or did he know that a gift offered would beget other gifts? This small inadequate offering was made to let the group rest. And this tired, parched group rose to the occasion. How miraculous is that?

How often have I held back my gifts, thinking them embarrassingly inadequate, thinking that those around me are too poor (in spirit or gifts) to rise to the occasion. Or more likely, thinking that those around me should rise to the occasion, but probably won't and I'll get stuck doing it all. If I do offer my help, I do so hoping for a reciprocal offering and not really believing that my help is enough. But perhaps it is. Perhaps what I have just needs to be offered. And perhaps it will be enough and we can all rest.

A Savior

John 4:4-30
And He had to pass through Samaria. So He came to a city of Samaria called Sychar, near the parcel of ground that Jacob gave to his son Joseph; and Jacob's well was there. So Jesus, being wearied from His journey, was sitting thus by the well. It was about the sixth hour.

There came a woman of Samaria to draw water. Jesus said to her, "Give Me a drink." For His disciples had gone away into the city to buy food. Therefore the Samaritan woman said to Him, "How is it that you, being a Jew, ask me for a drink since I am a Samaritan woman?" (For Jews have no dealings with Samaritans.) Jesus answered and said to her, "If you knew the gift of God, and who it is who says to you, 'Give Me a drink,' you would have asked Him, and He would have given you living water." She said to Him, "Sir, You have nothing to draw with and the well is deep; where then do you get that living water? You are not greater than our father Jacob, are you, who gave us the well, and drank of it himself and his sons and his cattle?" Jesus answered and said to her, "Everyone who drinks of this water will thirst again; but whoever drinks of the water that I will give him shall never thirst; but the water that I will give him will become in him a well of water springing up to eternal life." The woman said to Him, "Sir, give me this water, so I will not be thirsty nor come all the way here to draw."

He said to her, "Go, call your husband and come here." The woman answered and said, "I have no husband." Jesus said to her, "You have correctly said, 'I have no husband'; for you have had five husbands, and the one whom you now have is not your husband; this you have said truly."

The woman said to Him, "Sir, I perceive that you are a prophet. Our fathers worshiped in this mountain, and you people say that in Jerusalem is the place where men ought to worship." Jesus said to her, "Woman, believe me, an hour is coming when neither in this mountain nor in Jerusalem will you worship the Father. You worship what you do not know; we worship what we know, for salvation is from the Jews. "But an hour is coming, and now is, when the true worshipers will worship the Father in spirit and truth; for such people the Father seeks to be His worshipers. God is spirit, and those who worship Him must worship in spirit and truth." The woman said to Him, "I know that Messiah is coming (He who is called Christ); when that One comes, He will declare all things to us." Jesus said to her, "I who speak to you am He."

At this point His disciples came, and they were amazed that He had been speaking with a woman, yet no one said, "What do You seek?" or, "Why do You speak with her?" So the woman left her water pot, and went into the city and said to the men, "Come, see a man who told me all the things that I have done; this is not the Christ, is it?"

They went out of the city, and were coming to Him.

To a lonely woman with five ex-husbands and a tiring job of carrying water...
    A kind man who knows her past and still offers friendship
        is a savior.

To a town full of people in the doldrums of daily routines and chores...
    An excited woman with a message of hope
        is a savior.

To a land torn by rules of conduct and hierarchy of worth...
    An honest exchange between warring factions
        is a saving act.

To the thirsty in hot weather with rare deep wells...
    Gathering water is a saving act.
    Sharing water is a healing act.

Don't wait for a savior to come.
The savior is the one talking to you… here… now.

Let us offer friendship.
    Let us share our hope.
        Let us talk over the walls.
            Let us gather water and share it with our neighbors.

May we all be saviors.
We need all we can get.

Just Talk

Also on John 4:4-30

Jesus
Jew
Woman
Samaritan
All misunderstood.
So much tension. So much division.
For so long.
Jews don't talk to Samaritans.
Women don't converse with men who aren't their husbands.
So long...
Still it lasts.
Who can worship in Jerusalem?
Who must worship elsewhere?
Who owns Jerusalem?
Who owns women?
The well is so deep.
The water is so hard to get.
No bucket.
Do the Jews hold the secret to the Living Water?
Do the Christians?
Do those who worship outside Jerusalem?
Who is savior?
Is it Jesus?
Is it a woman?
What will save us?
Living water?
How do we get it?
We just have to talk to each other.

Someone to Lean On

Matthew 17:14-23
And when they were come to the multitude, there came to him a certain man, kneeling down to him, and saying, Lord, have mercy on my son: for he is lunatic, and sore vexed: for ofttimes he falleth into the fire, and oft into the water. And I brought him to thy disciples, and they could not cure him. Then Jesus answered and said, O faithless and perverse generation, how long shall I be with you? How long shall I suffer you? Bring him hither to me. And Jesus rebuked the devil; and he departed out of him: and the child was cured from that very hour. Then came the disciples to Jesus apart, and said, "Why could not we cast him out?" And Jesus said unto them, Because of your unbelief: for verily I say unto you, If ye have faith as a grain of mustard seed, ye shall say unto this mountain, and it shall remove; and nothing shall be impossible unto you. Howbeit this kind goes not out but by prayer and fasting. And while they abode in Galilee, Jesus said unto them, The Son of man shall be betrayed into the hands of men: And they shall kill him and the third day he shall be raised again. And they were exceedingly sorry.

I miss my Dad. He was a problem solver. When I called with a problem, he usually had really good advice, especially when it had to do with money. When my eyes glazed over reading insurance forms or a retirement fund prospectus, he could explain it to me in terms I could understand and guide me in a good direction. I leaned on Dad for help in these matters. And now he is gone.

When he got cancer, he knew he would die soon, so he spent time helping me learn the things I would need to know after he was gone. But I still miss him. And I wish I'd paid just a bit more attention when he was explaining things. But for a long time, he was always there. And now he is gone.

And now I have people who lean on me. Family, friends, employees. I enjoy sharing my experiences, passing along the good advice others passed to me, and making people happy. It makes me feel good. I like to think my help gets rid of a demon here or there. But how long will I be with them? And what then?

Sometimes I just get tired. I want Dad back to field this problem. I want the ones that lean on me to do it themselves once in a while. And I think, if they would try, just a bit, they would find it isn't all that hard. The faith of a mustard seed. That's all. Give me a break today. I remind them that I won't be around forever and I encourage them to try. And that makes them sad. But sometimes that little bit of push does the trick. They remember the instructions I gave them last time. They feel an urgency to learn – before I am gone. And sure enough, they do handle it themselves this time. The seed begins to grow. So, a new strong tree will be there, when I am gone, for others to lean on, at least for a time.

Stuff

Matthew 19:16-26
Then someone came to him and said, "Teacher, what good deed must I do to have eternal life?" And he said to him, "Why do you ask me about what is good? There is only one who is good. If you wish to enter into life, keep the commandments." He said to him, "Which ones?" And Jesus said, "You shall not murder; You shall not commit adultery: You shall not steal: You shall not bear false witness; Honor your father and mother; also. You shall love your neighbor as yourself." The young man said to him, "I have kept all these; what do I still lack?" Jesus said to him, "If you wish to be perfect, so, sell your possessions, and give the money to the poor, and you will have treasure in heaven; then come, follow me." When the young man heard this word, he went away grieving, for he had many possessions. Then Jesus said to his disciples, "Truly I tell you, it will be hard for a rich person to enter the kingdom of heaven. Again I tell you, it is easier for a camel to go through the eye of a needle than for someone who is rich to enter the kingdom of God." When the disciples heard this, they were greatly astounded and said, "Then who can be saved?" But Jesus looked at them and said, "For mortals it is impossible, but for God all things are possible."

I'm sitting in a coffee shop, "skinny" vanilla latte in front of me, working at my laptop computer. I don't consider myself rich, but I do enjoy many of life's comforts. So I'm afraid that, according to Jesus, I am far from perfect, though closer than I once was. I lost half of my possessions in a divorce. It was an amicable separation, but there was still a need to divide the loot. Technology allowed us both to keep all the music on I-Tunes. But everything else got divided up. It was hard, sorting through everything we owned, allowing the Kurt Vonnegut books, the video of "American Beauty" and treasured Christmas decorations to be packed into boxes and taken away. There are "things" that I was sure I would miss. But the odd thing is that, aside from a book here and there, I don't really miss the things that went away with him. I went from a three-bedroom house to a one-bedroom apartment. My possessions were not sold, though much did go to Goodwill. But my ability to downsize surprised me. With the move went specialized appliances (bread maker, waffle iron, crepe maker) I had seldom used, books I had already read (or just read the first chapter and then lost interest), clothes I had out grown. I actually appreciated reducing the amount of seemingly endless Tupperware containers that had accumulated in 25 years of marriage. I imagine that they are all now in good homes with people who appreciate them more than I did.

I now live in a 2-bedroom apartment that I share with my new love. Much of his former "stuff" went to furnish the homes of his two now-grown children, which is a good thing since our apartment does not have a basement or an attic in which to store extraneous items. We can't keep accumulating in our limited space. We have to evaluate our holdings fairly often and decide what is worthy to take up space. Last week we sent three grocery bags of books to the library's used-book sale. There are things that I am not willing to give up, my computer being at the top of that list. Sometimes I am struck by the number of things that clutter my space simply because I have grown attached to them. A vase given to me by an artist friend. The handy caddy that holds a host of really cool (though seldom-used) cooking utensils. Rocks from every beach I've ever been to. A digital camera that lets me share photos of my grandson with my Mom who is too far away to visit often. The macramé hanging that has hung in every dwelling I have occupied since college. Can I really be expected to give these things up? And for what? What really would be the point of giving it all up? I refuse to believe that whatever God there may be expects this of us.

But I have to admit that with the reduction of stuff, I gained perspective. The whole analysis process helped me look at the things I owned with new eyes. I do miss the cat that moved with my ex, and friends who also moved with him. But stuff is just stuff. Despite the call to sell it all, in our culture and weather, we do have a physical need for a few things. And I feel quite justified in hanging on to those.

I have come to appreciate the odd collection of recycled furniture that graces our home. The artwork on the walls recalls times with friends or fun excursions. We have a functional set of dishes, sheets, towels, and cookware. Of course we have our technical toys (laptop, digital camera, iPod, and DVR) that I am way too attached to.

Matthew was right. It is impossible for us mere mortals to sell all, to be perfect. I don't think we're able to do it. But we can take steps. And what would replace the stuff? Maybe, after we got through whining about the inconvenience of it all, we'd be more in touch with the world around us – nature, friends, weather, feelings. Maybe we'd notice the needs of other people, those who don't have even the basics. Maybe we'd have more time to teach children about the arts. Maybe we'd make a mark on the world, make it a better place for future generations. Maybe we'd discover the kingdom of God.

Prayer

Matthew 21:21-22
Jesus answered and said unto them, Verily I say unto you, If ye have faith, and doubt not, if ye shall say unto this mountain, Be thou removed, and be thou cast into the sea; it shall be done. And all things, whatsoever ye ask in prayer, believing, ye shall receive.

When I was young, a classmate had problems that doctors, at that time, did not know how to fix. She always seemed upset and irrational. As she grew older, she seemed childishly afraid and self-centered. Her parents tried many things, but nothing seemed to work. I felt sorry for her and her parents, so I prayed for them a lot.

"Whatsoever ye ask in prayer, believing, ye shall receive."

I believed. I really did. And I prayed fervently. I prayed that she would be happy. I prayed that her parents would experience some relief from the constant stress. But she continued without improvement. She called the police on her family. She was asked to leave school for disruptive behavior. And still she seemed sad.

One day, a well-meaning person from my church declared, "You obviously don't have enough faith. If you did, she would be healed." It was the beginning of a downward spiral for me, away from church, away from scripture. What did this person know of my faith? I had not prayed that this girl would move away or be cast into the sea (though there were times I thought either of those would be a good solution.) I prayed for her to be happy. I imagined her happy, no longer jealous of everyone around her. I imagined her being appreciative of the many people who tried to help her. I imagined her using her many talents to bless the world around her. I felt that my prayer was unselfish and honorable. And I truly believed it was possible for God to answer this prayer.

But God didn't. Last I knew, she was still unhappy, jealous, paranoid, and disruptive. This mountain did not move. But I do believe the prayer helped me. I found other people with similar unanswered prayers: good people, many of them with tremendous faith, long-suffering and generous, still praying. What I learned from them is that the prayer, not the answer, is the blessing.

Looking at a mountain can be a terrifying experience. My own limitations come crashing in on me as I view the immensity of the mountain. And I freeze, sometimes unable to move forward. But prayer changes that.

When I see a mountain ahead, and I ask that the mountain be removed, I have seldom experienced any movement by the mountain; certainly no casting into the sea kind of movement. But my prayer helps me recognize the mountain for what it is. It is both an obstacle and a goal. I am afraid of the cliffs, the jagged rocks, the icy peaks. But I want to see from the top, to experience the thrill of having overcome my fears, to see things from a new perspective.

The prayer brings all these things into focus. The prayer allows me to move ahead. Sometimes I find a path around the mountain. Sometimes I gear up for the trek, and in doing so, find fellow travelers who know the secret to a successful climb. Sometimes I realize that getting past this particular mountain is really not all that important to me. And I move off in another direction, only (of course) to encounter a different mountain, but this time one I care about scaling.

Sometimes the mountain is dealing with a difficult person. Sometimes it is depression. Sometimes it is a dying parent. For me, in spite of my prayers, the mountains do not move. Maybe they never will. Maybe I don't believe enough. Maybe the mountain doesn't want to move. But, through prayer, I do believe I will find support, resolution, strength, and peace.
Amen.

What's Love Got to do with it?

Matthew 22:35-40
Then one of them, which was a lawyer, asked him a question, tempting him, and saying, Master, which is the great commandment in the law? Jesus said unto him, "Thou shalt love the Lord thy God with all thy heart, and with all thy soul, and with all thy mind. This is the first and great commandment. And the second is like unto it, Thou shalt love thy neighbor as thyself. On these two commandments hang all the law and the prophets."

I had a root canal yesterday and my mouth hurts. I hadn't intended to spend my day in the dentist's chair, but that's the way things go sometimes. Between the dentist and the endodontist, I took calls from my Mom (computer questions), my husband (the water pipes at work were leaking again), and my office (how should we record subscriber payments). I got emails from my sister (how do you deal with an unreasonable collections agency), an Internet store (my order has been delayed), and the church (please sign up to help with the Bazaar).

I'm just trying to get through my day, keep the wheels turning on my life, fulfill my responsibilities. What's love got to do with it? What does that mean, Love the Lord, thy God? And what if I do? What then? No one is saying, "Let me take care of you." I'm sitting at the right hand of my boss, my Mom, my sister, my husband, and my friends helping us all get through life. What does it mean to love God, and why is it so important? Frankly, it makes my head hurt to think about this. I have other things to deal with today, things that demand my immediate attention. I don't have time for love right now. Perhaps I will later. But not today. I have computer problems at work and a house to clean when I get home. Don't make me stop and think about love. Not now. Maybe later, when my mouth quits hurting and things slow down at work.

But maybe love is just what I need right now.

Maybe what I need is to take a few minutes, right now, to think about love.

OK. I'm thinking.

Is love the same as admiration? Or appreciation?
I love nature, the beautiful trees with graceful branches and whole ecosystems alive inside them. I love the clouds that dance above my head, even those that bring rain or lightening. And this beauty is there every day, whether or not I notice. Is my love of God's creation the same as loving the Lord thy God?

Is love reverence?
I certainly am in awe of the intricate web of existence of which I am a part. I am in awe of the huge part of that web that I suspect is there, but I can't even begin to comprehend. Galaxies and far off stars that I will never see. Is that love?

I care. Is that love?
When I try to provide a good work environment for my employees, to be a good employee myself, is that a form of love? I try to be a good daughter, a good sister, a good wife, a good grandmother, a good friend. Is that love? Is that love for God or for my neighbor? Is that why the two laws are together at the top of the list?

But love with all my heart, with all my mind, with all my soul? Even when my mouth hurts? Even when I'm crazy busy? That's going to be hard. I'm not sure I can do that.

So I think I'm going to try to stop and pay attention to love, whatever that may be, once a day. That shouldn't be so very hard. And I know I can find something to love, something to recognize as God, once a day. And that will be a good start.

God Forgives

Luke 23:34
Then said Jesus, "Father, forgive them; for they know not what they do."

I said something. At the time, it seemed so ordinary. I didn't mean anyone any harm. I just made a statement. But it offended someone. Actually, it offended several someones. And now things are different.

I have told the story of what happened to many people now. My version of the story makes it quite clear that I was innocent of any wrongdoing. My comment came from my background, my understanding of the situation, my viewpoint. But my comment fell on ears of those whose backgrounds, understanding, and views were different from mine.

I truly didn't mean any harm. And when I found out that they were upset, I apologized. But I did not say what they wanted me to say. And they have never forgiven me.

That happened five years ago. And it still hurts.

In those five years, the story of my comment spread and grew. I explained – again – that I did not make the statement maliciously. I admitted that I was ignorant and insensitive. I apologized. I said that I had learned from my mistake and would not do it again. But it didn't matter. I still was not forgiven.

And five years after the offending utterance, I find myself still wanting to do something to fix it. Perhaps another explanation; another apology. But instead of offering forgiveness, they offer only punishment. I feel unjustly crucified. They want me to admit that I had angry, unjust, or arrogant thoughts when I said it. But I was just dumb and insensitive. And I want more than anything to be forgiven. Forgive me, for I knew not what I was doing.

It strikes me now that I have not forgiven them, either. After five years, I am still angry at how unfairly they treated me. Maybe they, coming as they do from a different viewpoint, don't know how much they have hurt me. Maybe I need to forgive them. This makes my head hurt.

In our congregation at St. Nicholas, at the beginning of Great Lent, we celebrate Forgiveness Sunday. Each congregant faces each other congregant one at a time. Each says, "Forgive me." And each responds with "God forgives." It is a really amazing experience. Though we ask each person present for forgiveness, no one has to admit to a failing and no one has to say "I forgive you." But I face each person, wondering whether or not I've offended them; wondering how much forgiveness I need. And the answer comes back the same each time. God forgives.

I don't know who or what God is or how God's forgiveness works. But I believe that we have the ability to recover from our mistakes, even those that other people fail to forgive, even those of others that I have not forgiven. I think that we need to believe that there is forgiveness, somewhere in the universe. Forgiveness from God that comes as a part of nature, even when we don't know we need it. Forgiveness that opens our eyes to the needs around us, encourages us to forgive others, heals our own wounds and allows us to grow, if only we will accept it.

God forgives.

Invitations

Matthew 22:1-14
And Jesus answered and spoke unto them again by parables, and said, The kingdom of heaven is like unto a certain king, which made a marriage for his son, and sent forth his servants to call them that were bidden to the wedding: and they would not come. Again, he sent forth other servants, saying, Tell them which are bidden, "Behold, I have prepared my dinner: my oxen and my fatlings are killed, and all things are ready: come unto the marriage." But they made light of it, and went their ways, one to his farm, another to his merchandise: And the remnant took his servants, and entreated them spitefully, and slew them. But when the king heard thereof, he was wroth: and he sent forth his armies, and destroyed those murderers, and burned up their city. Then said he to his servants," The wedding is ready, but they, which were bidden, were not worthy. Go ye therefore into the highways, and as many as ye shall find, bid to the marriage." So those servants went out into the highways, and gathered together all as many as they found, both bad and good: and the wedding was furnished with guests. And when the king came in to see the guests, he saw there a man which had not on a wedding garment: And he said unto him, Friend, how came thou in hither not having a wedding garment? And he was speechless. Then said the king to the servants, Bind him hand and foot, and take him away and cast him into outer darkness; there shall be weeping and gnashing of teeth. For many are called, but few are chosen.

I'm sitting in Starbucks listening to John Lennon sing *"I call your name, but you're not there."* I feel sad as I read that this king cannot get people to attend his son's wedding. The invited were offered good food and a good time, but it was not enough to make them take time from their busy schedule. When the servants went back with promises of more goodies, they were actually killed. "Leave us alone. We said we don't want to attend, but you came back. How dare you!" What is wrong with these people?

Upon first glance, I have no experience to equate to this story. I certainly have not killed any messengers. I have rejected wedding invitations, but no one cared enough about my presence to ask twice. And who in their right mind would reject the kingdom of heaven?

I have been asked to walk for AIDS, but it was hot that day and I really needed to do laundry. I was asked to teach the Sunday School class, but I was sure someone else would volunteer. I hated to give up my free Saturday to prepare class materials. That time they did come back and ask again. But I deleted the email. I could pretend I didn't get it. I am asked regularly to contribute money for medical research, food for the hungry, nature preservation, housing for the homeless, and other good causes.

John Lennon repeats, "I call your name. But you're not there. Was I to blame for being unfair?"

Pitifully little of my money goes for these things, but I have not given up my latte, my laptop, or my cable TV. I like my lifestyle, and although I protest it is not extravagant, it is comfortable.

Is it possible that if I accepted the invitation to give money, to teach children, to support good causes with my presence that the kingdom of heaven would be closer to reality? Is it possible that, if a lot of people answered the call, the kingdom of heaven would actually exist? I'm not sure. Human nature being what it is, our culture's deep commitment to material acquisition, and the frantic pace of our lives makes it hard to think very far into the future and makes me doubt the possibility of a "kingdom of heaven" here on earth.

I'm tired. My faith in the ability to cure AIDS or make a dent in eliminating poverty is pretty close to non-existent. Why go to the wedding? It's false hope for an impossible vision. Maybe I have killed the messengers.

John Lennon continues, "You know I can't take it. I don't know who can. I'm not going to make it. I'm not that kind of man."

The fact is that the wedding went on without the naysayers and murderers. Others, the second string if you will, gathered at the wedding and ate great food and danced with the bride. They came prepared to participate in a wedding and experienced, even if just for a day, the fruits of that participation. The man who tried to crash the wedding, unprepared but wanting the benefits, was not allowed to stay. The second-stringers experienced a little bit of heaven. Like the murderers in the story who were killed by the king, maybe I have experienced a sort of spiritual death, a retribution for my lack of participation and faith.

John Lennon is still singing. "You know I can't sleep at night, but just the same, I never weep at night. I call your name."

The invitations are still coming. What if I occasionally responded positively? What would it hurt? I'm still not convinced that there can ever be "world peace," but I do believe there can be pockets of heaven here on earth. And I'd really like to experience a few.

Saving a Soul

Mark 8:34-38
Whosoever will come after me, let him deny himself, and take up his cross, and follow me. For whosoever will save his life shall lose it; but whosoever shall lose his life for my sake and the gospel's, the same shall save it. For what shall it profit a man, if he shall gain the whole world, and lose his own soul? Or what shall a man give in exchange for his soul?

Deny myself.
Take up my cross.
Follow.
Save my life and lose it.
Lose my life and save it.

Just wordplay,
Religious propaganda.
My defenses are up.
I don't want to deny myself.
I'm not really a follower.
Why should I change my path?
Just because I feel lost?
The world is what it is.
Being lost is just part of the deal.
Don't try to save my soul.
Not everyone wants to do things your way.

Deny myself.
Take up my cross.
I take another look.
Deny myself AND take up my cross.
I don't have to give up all that is me.
I get to keep my concerns, my loves, my soul.
My cross.

Just don't weigh the cross down with things,
With fear of change,
With protective walls.

So, here I am with my cross,
unprotected and vulnerable.
Now what?

Follow.
Others have gone before who have carried these same burdens.
There is wisdom out there that can lighten my load.
Follow ideas, not possessions.
Build bridges, not walls.
Learn new ways.
Hard work.
Is it worth it?

Save my life.
Instead of preserving my way of life,
protecting what is mine;
Instead of saving my life,
I will try to look beyond what "is"
to what "might be,"
To lose my comfortable life.

I will follow the wisdom of the ages,
Move in new directions,
Bear the cross that is my life with all its ups and downs.
Notice what is working, what needs to change.
Recognize that nothing is worth protecting
Except my soul.

Lose my old life.
Save my soul.
A good trade.

Winter

Luke 21:28-33
And when these things begin to come to pass, then look up, and lift up your heads; for your redemption draws nigh. And he spoke to them a parable; Behold the fig tree, and all the trees; when they now shoot forth ye see and know of your own selves that summer is now nigh at hand. So likewise ye, when ye see these things come to pass, know ye that the kingdom of God is nigh at hand. Verify I say unto you, this generation shall not pass away till all is fulfilled. Heaven and earth shall pass away; but my words shall not pass away.

It is cold outside. Yes, even in Berkeley, California, it gets cold. People are bundled up with scarves and hats and even gloves. The higher altitudes got snow last night. It is a time of year when we try not to be outside any more than necessary. My mom, who lives in Chicago, is avoiding the icy roads and slippery sidewalks, not wanting to repeat her fall of last winter that required hip surgery. Our attention is focused on staying safe and warm. We really aren't paying a lot of attention to the trees except perhaps to notice they have lost their leaves. Spring seems a long way off. There is no need to look for signs of spring. Just keep warm. Maybe sleep a bit.

I drive home from work in the dark. When I get home, I turn up the heat and cook something warm for dinner. I settle into the couch to watch my favorite TV shows, under my TV blanket. My cat climbs into my lap. I blush to admit that when the news comes on, I turn the TV off and prepare for bed. I'm feeling enough stress right now. My efforts are directed to family and Christmas preparations. I have no energy for the outside world. My energy is turned inward. Keeping warm.

But there are signs out there. Signs that change is imminent, happening even now. Signs that I need to change. For my redemption is nigh. But I just want to sleep and keep warm. Redemption really isn't a high priority for me right now.

Perhaps, when it gets a bit warmer, I will notice the changes; stronger from my winter's nap. Maybe then I will have regained some strength to see the fig tree sprouts. And perhaps I will be able to attend to them, to help this new life along. To nurture the kingdom of God even as it sprouts in the midst of a cold and dangerous world. When I have recovered from my dormant, internal hiatus, I will see the signs and can take up the cause.

But right now, I just need to stay warm.
And sleep.

Resurrection

Luke 20:27-38
Then came to him certain of the Sadducees, which deny that there is any resurrection: and they asked him, Saying, Master, Moses wrote unto us, If any man's brother die, having a wife, and he die without children, that his brother should take his wife, and raise up seed unto his brother.... Therefore in resurrection whose wife of them is she? And Jesus answering said unto them, The children of this world marry, and are given in marriage: But they which shall be accounted worthy to obtain that world, and the resurrection from the dead, neither marry, nor are given in marriage: Neither can they die any more: for they are equal unto the angels; and are the children of God, being the children of the resurrection. Now that the dead are raised, even Moses showed at the bush, when he called the Lord the God of Abraham, and the God of Isaac, and the God of Jacob. For he is not a God of the dead, but of the living: for all live unto him.

Last year Michael and I got married. It was the second marriage for both of us. My first marriage ended in divorce. Michael's wife died. Cancer. He loved her until she died, and then some. This year my Dad died. He and Mom were married for 57 years and my Mom talks of the time when she will be with him again. And I wonder, what of me? The fact that I really don't know what lies beyond this life, and truly believe it is not within our grasp to understand, makes this question rather silly. But I think it anyway. In resurrection, who will get Michael? I reluctantly theorize that Priscilla should. Together they had two children, 30 years of marriage, her whole adult life. And then I wonder why I am spending my time in this useless exercise. We don't know what happens. But the thought still creeps in from time to time.

After Michael and I had been together for two years, we were driving through the town where Priscilla was buried. Michael suggested that we stop. I hadn't realized we were in the vicinity, and without time to think, I agreed. We wound through the cemetery roads to a patch of low stones where Pricilla's grave was located. The grave was overgrown with weeds and we both knelt to pull them away. In silence we cleared the stone and the area around. When we stood, Michael quietly spoke. "Priscilla, meet Joy. Joy, Priscilla." It was such an amazing moment. We both stood with tears running down our cheeks. I felt a connection to Michael and to his life that I had not felt before. In this moment, there was no competition, no winner, no loser. Just a profound sense of love. There was resurrection for all of us. Michael and I had both risen from the despair of love lost. And Priscilla lived on, not as an obstacle to our love, but as a testament to the ability to love. I experienced the God of the living, even as we paid tribute to the dead.

The God of the dead is beyond our comprehension and theorizing about "who gets the girl" in the life hereafter is really not very productive. But we can know the God of the living. We experience that God in the inner strength that sees us through our dark times, in the care that others bestow when we are fragile, through the little moments that connect us beyond our expectations, and within the memories of lives well lived. And this God of living brings resurrection and hope to our lives.

Special thanks to:
Michael Peterson
Kit and John Wright
Susan McKibbon
Father Stephan Meholik
Dr. Carolyn Pressler
Sheryl Coryell
John Handley
Jennifer Ryu
Dorothy Troyer

www.ingramcontent.com/pod-product-compliance
Lightning Source LLC
Chambersburg PA
CBHW071831290426
44109CB00017B/1800